D0936522

The
Beatles
Reader

ROCK & ROLL REMEMBRANCES *SERIES*

ROCK & ROLL REFERENCE *SERIES*

pierian press
1984

The
Beatles
Reader

A Selection of Contemporary
Views, News & Reviews of
The Beatles In Their Heyday

edited by

Charles P. Neises

ISBN 0-87650-170-6
LC 84-60267

THE PIERIAN PRESS
Post Office Box 1808
Ann Arbor, MI 48106

Contents

From Fleet Street to Wall Street, the Beatles were
big news. What were they really like? How much
money did they make? What did they think about
religion? Five articles deal with the Beatles' first visit
to the United States, John Lennon's statement
about the relative popularity of the group and Jesus
Christ, their trip to Rishikesh, India, and the Paul
McCartney death hoax.
The Beatles recorded several albums that are still
considered classics of the rock-and-roll genre. Three
of these works, **Rubber Soul, Sergeant Pepper's
Lonely Hearts Club Band** and **The Beatles**, are dis-
sected by a music professor, a poetry scholar and a
rock historian.

Introduction

My private search for material written about the Beatles reminds me of the story of the man who tried to record the events of one day in history. Out of convenience he chose the day before, but as he exhausted source after source, "the day before" drifted into history by weeks and then by months. He learned foreign languages and bought stacks of old newspapers in his search for facts about that one day. He died several years later knowing more about that single day than any other man, but he still had not learned everything. An entire universe happened on that day, and no single man can know a universe.

Although the body of works on the Beatles hardly constitutes a universe, it can seem equally imposing. The average reader needs only to visit the local bookstore to see that the selection of books in print about a rock-and-roll group disbanded for over ten years is still formidable. Recent events concerning individual members of the group have prompted publishers to add to the total with publications of varying quality. Paul McCartney's 1976 American tour with Wings primed the market for a handful of souvenir books and upbeat histories of the Beatles. And the murder of John Lennon in 1980 caused a spate of mournful and sentimental paperback tributes.

The more adventurous Beatles reader can find old magazine articles waiting to be discovered in public and university libraries. The *Reader's Guide to Periodical Literature* lists over 100 articles from popular American magazines, covering the band's seven years as an international recording act. Among these is the first mention of the Beatles in an American magazine of general readership, a *Time* article from November 15, 1963, titled "The New Madness," reporting on their appearance at the Royal Variety Performance before the Queen Mother and Princess Margaret. At the time, few Americans had even heard of the Beatles, and the article avoids the image-related phrases ("cheeky," "mop-topped") that would later obscure their individual personalities. Thus the young Beatles reader (and the old Beatles reader who did not notice at the time) can survey those first, mixed appraisals of the Beatles by the American popular press. For the even more dedicated reader, the *Music Index* lists 130 articles from musical trade newspapers, for 1964 alone! The Beatles universe expands.

As this universe expands, the original fans grow older. The kids who were ten to sixteen years old when John, Paul, George and Ringo first hit the United States in 1964 are now twenty-seven to thirty-three years old and represent a constantly increasing reading level among Beatles readers. Those kids who read *Datebook* and *Tiger Beat* probably did not bother with mom and dad's copy of *Ramparts* or *National Review*, even if it did contain an article about the Beatles. By doing so they may have missed some of the more nimble-minded evaluations of the Beatles and their music.

In *The Beatles Reader* I have gathered some of those thoughtful writings from magazines and books of the last two decades. Some are reactions by contemporary critics of the 1960s; others are reevaluations by writers of the 1970s. Divided into five sections as they pertain to the Beatles as a group ("Beatles in the News," "Three Albums," "Varied Critical Viewpoints," "Two Movies" and "Beatlemania in the Seventies"), the readings offer points of view more varied than those found in "fanzine" articles and paperback biographies. In limiting the subject to the Beatles as a group, I have omitted articles dealing with their lives and their solo careers after 1970. Even a personal universe must have boundaries.

A book like this has been attempted once before. In 1968 the Cowles Education Corporation published *The Beatles Book*, a collection of fourteen articles edited by Edward E. Davis. The anthology addressed the permanence of the Beatles and signaled a new era of serious study of their music. But the best articles in *The Beatles Book* are products of the year following the release of the LP **Sergeant Pepper's Lonely Hearts Club Band** and treat the Beatles' major musical achievement of the time as their only achievement. The editor and contributors are not to be criticized for that; **Sergeant Pepper** was the overwhelming work that attracted the attention of "serious" commentators and more than deserved a book of its own. *The Beatles Reader* is, however, the first Beatles anthology compiled with the luxury of having the entire history of the Beatles as a group in the past. The boundaries here are marked out more clearly than they were for Mr. Davis.

This book is not a primer on the subject of the Beatles; for that purpose I suggest one of three books: *The Beatles* (originally subtitled "The Authorized Biography," McGraw-Hill, 1968, revised 1978) by Hunter Davies; *The Beatles Forever* (McGraw-Hill, 1978) by Nicholas Schaffner; or *Shout! The Beatles in Their Generation* (Fireside, 1981) by Philip Norman. If anything, *The Beatles Reader* is a primer on Beatles reading, demonstrating the variety of available sources and displaying some of the best writings from these sources. Beatles readers are those people interested enough in the group not only to buy new books and magazines but to locate old and out-of-print material from the relatively vast Beatles universe.

Young people, when they are obsessed with a popular movement such as a rock-and-roll group, are often said to be in a world of their own. Because of the wealth of material about the Beatles, their fans are not in a world of their own. They are in a universe of their own. As testimony to this, the first edition of a work called *Here, There and Everywhere: The First International Beatles Bibliography, 1962–1982*, soon to be published by Pierian Press, will contain about 8,000 citations to books, magazines, articles and reviews relating to the Beatles. The text of the book will be generated from a computerized database maintained by Pierian Press, which intends to continue to expand its automated files and publish successive editions of this work in future years.

C.P.N.
January, 1984

Acknowledgements

Carl Belz, "Rock and Fine Art." Reprinted with permission of the author.

David Bowman, "Scenarios for the Revolution in Pepperland." Reprinted with permission of the Editors of the *Journal of Popular Film and Television* from Volume 1, Number 3 of the *Journal of Popular Film.*

Ralph Brauer, "Iconic Modes: The Beatles." Reprinted from *Icons of America*, edited by Ray Browne and Marshall Fishwick, with permission of the Bowling Green State University Popular Press, Bowling Green, Ohio.

William F. Buckley, "The Beatles and the Guru." Reprinted with permission from *National Review*, March 12, 1968.

Abram Chasins, "High-Brows vs. No-Brows." Reprinted by permission of the McCall Publishing Company, from *McCall's*, September 1965.

Jonathan Cott, "A Hard Day's Knights." Reprinted with permission of the author.

David Frost, "John's Gospel." Reprinted with permission from *Spectator*, August 12, 1966.

John Gabree, "The Beatles in Perspective." Reprinted with permission of *Down Beat*.

"Hiram's Report." Reprinted by permission; © 1964 The New Yorker Magazine, Inc.

Steven Holroyd, "The Second Golden Age of Pop." Reprinted with permission of *Melody Maker*.

Jerry Lazar, "Magical History Tour." Reprinted with permission of the author.

Lilith Moon, "Beatlemaniacs Never Die (But They Sure Get Carried Away)." Copyright © 1974 by *Creem*. Reprinted from *Creem*, November 1974.

Terence J. O'Grady, "The Ballad Style in the Early Music of the Beatles." Reprinted with permission from *College Music Symposium*, Volume 29, Number 1, 1979.

Terence J. O'Grady, " 'Rubber Soul' and the Social Dance Tradition." Reprinted with permission from *Ethnomusicology*, January 1979.

Vance Packard, "Building the Beatle Image." Reprinted from *The Saturday Evening Post* © 1964 The Curtis Publishing Company.

David R. Pichaske, "Sustained Performances: Sergeant Pepper's Lonely Hearts Club Band." Reprinted with permission of Macmillan Publishing Co., Inc. from *Beowulf to Beatles: Approaches to Poetry* by David R. Pichaske. Copyright © 1972 by The Free Press, a Division of Macmillan Publishing Co., Inc.

Richard Poirier, "Learning from the Beatles." From *The Performing Self: Compositions and Decompositions in the Languages of Contemporary Life* by Richard Poirier. Copyright © 1971 by Oxford University Press, Inc. Reprinted by permission.

Patrick Snyder, "People and Things That Went Before." Reprinted with permission of the author.

Thank you, folks

Lots of thanks to everyone who helped and offered support and encouragement: Prof. RW, PL, RR, MS, GM, P+DG, SH (+KE), CS, MG, JH, DH, SS, Sr. JA-N, the Basics, Mm, Dd, and Julie.

Part I
Beatles in the News

Introduction to
HIRAM'S REPORT

Whether or not he was a real teenage nephew of a real *New Yorker* operative, Hiram Stanley wrote three articles about the Beatles for that magazine in 1964. The first, reprinted here, chronicles the Beatles' first visit to New York City for appearances on the "Ed Sullivan Show" and a concert at Carnegie Hall. Hiram concludes that the group is good, but not as good as the Everly Brothers. In the second, "A Report from Hiram" (*The New Yorker*, August 22, 1964, pages 25–27), he reviews the New York premiere of "A Hard Day's Night" and announces that "the Beatles are going to be around for quite a while." In the third, "Hiram and the Animals" (*The New Yorker*, September 12, 1964, pages 40–43), he changes his allegiance to the Animals when *The House of the Rising Sun* knocks *A Hard Day's Night* from the number one position according to the September 2, 1964, *Variety*.

The fickle Hiram was never heard from again.

HIRAM'S REPORT

by Hiram Stanley

A bulky manuscript in a bold cursive hand appeared on our desk the other morning. A label on it read "BEATLES," and attached to it was a typewritten note from our operative Mr. Stanley. Stanley wrote, "Craven apologies. Fell disease, of cause unknown, has laid up yours truly. Have pressed into service teen-age nephew, Hiram. Forgive, if possible, his scientific approach; he is a coleopterist at heart. Regards, S."

Hiram wrote:

"HIRAM'S REPORT"

"SUBJECT: The Beatles.

"PURPOSE OF REPORT: To Tell Uncle All I Know About the Beatles in New York, which is quite a lot.

"READINGS: 'Musicologically . . . ' by Theodore Strongin, in the *Times*, February 10, 1964:

"The Beatles have a tendency to build phrases around unresolved leading tones. This precipitates the ear into a false modal frame that temporarily turns the fifth of the scale into the tonic, momentarily suggesting the mixolydian mode. But everything ends as plain diatonic all the same.

" 'Why They Go Wild Over the Beatles,' by Dr. Joyce Brothers, in the *Journal-American*, February 11, 1964:

"The Beatles display a few mannerisms which almost seem a shade on the feminine side, such as the tossing of their long manes of hair . . . . These are exactly the mannerisms which very young female fans (in the 10-to-14 age group) appear to go wildest over.

"*Variety*, February 12, 1964:

"The Beatles' asking price for a single evening is $7,000 against 60% of the gross. In addition, the promoters must supply a band and a surrounding show the entire half [*sic*] of the evening. In addition, the promoter has to lay out an advertising budget, pay for the hall, also pay stagehands, electricians, printing tickets, and sundry other items. The promoters feel that under these circumstances, it will be extremely difficult to make a buck.

"The Beatles have been selling phonograph disks worldwide at the monthly rate of $1,200,000. In less than a year, the boys, all in young 20's, have grossed about $12,000,000 before computing taxes, trade expenses, promotion and other costs.

"PROCEDURE: It being my aim to see as much of the Beatles as possible, I met them at Kennedy Airport on Friday, followed them around on Sunday, and attended the second of their two concerts at Carnegie Hall on Wednesday. This was quite a good deal of seeing of the Beatles in only six days.

"OBSERVATIONS: The Beatles got to the airport before I did, and had a drink, but I slipped into the pressroom before they could, and with much less fuss. There were lots of kids waiting outside the pressroom for a chance to scream at the Beatles (screaming at the Beatles is what they seem to want to do most), and they screamed at me a little when I went in — just to get warmed up, I guess. The pressroom was pretty full, and I squeezed into a spot over to the left, beside a lot of men who were there from English newspapers. Most of them, it turned out, had been in this country so long they had never seen the Beatles, but nevertheless they were all pretending to be bored by the Beatles. They said things like 'What's all this, then, Tony? What's it all abaht?' 'Oh, hullo, Frank, what are you writing?' 'I'm trying not to write anything, but I'm told I have to turn out some sort of squalid prose.'

"Just then, the kids outside really started screaming, so I was sure the Beatles would be in shortly, and they were. There were four of them, of course, and I couldn't yet tell them apart, but they were all dressed rather nicely, I thought. I counted three black suits, one gray suit, one white shirt, one gray shirt, two Tattersall shirts, three black ties, and one dark-blue tie. Also four pairs of black shoes. There was a lot of noise, and their press agent, Brian Somerville, got up and said, 'Ladies and gentlemen, this is ridiculous! Hold up your hands, and I'll recognize you one at a time. If you won't be quiet, we'll just stand here until you are.' He sounded like a teacher I know very well. Finally, there was a certain amount of quiet, and reporters asked questions and the Beatles gave some funny answers. They seemed to be enjoying themselves. When one reporter asked them, 'What are you going to do about all the car-bumper stickers in Detroit that say, "Stamp Out the Beatles"?' one Beatle said, 'We're printing some stickers that say, "Stamp Out Detroit".' Then a reporter asked, 'Are you part of a social rebellion against the older generation?' and a Beatle said, 'It's a dirty lie!' It was the right answer, too.

"On Sunday, the Beatles were on the 'Ed Sullivan Show' in the evening, and I went over to Ed Sullivan's studio, at Broadway and Fifty-third Street, in the afternoon to watch them rehearse. Outside were a number of kids in yellow sweatshirts that had 'WMCA Good Guys' printed on them (the Good Guys are a bunch of disc jockeys on that station who have been pushing the Beatles), and one boy had on a white sweatshirt on which he had written 'WQXR Bad Guys.' In the studio, the floor of the stage was painted blue, and there were some large white arrows pointing at a spot on it. I guessed that that was where the Beatles would sing, and I was right. Some orchestra members were tuning up onstage, others were standing around looking at the spot where the arrows were pointing, and also looking at the auditorium seats, which were filled with kids, dressed for a party and behaving themselves. The orchestra members who were standing around were trying to look the way the English reporters at the airport had been trying to look, only older and tireder. 'All peach fuzz,' said one of them, nodding at the kids. Then another one walked up and said, 'Look at all the peach fuzz.' They all seemed to be thinking the same thoughts. Then drums for the Beatle named Ringo were rolled onstage, and the kids, who had been quiet, suddenly began screaming. Orchestra members produced a few falsetto imitations of the kids. 'And these are the people who are going to be running the country twenty years from now!' said the man who had made the first peach-fuzz remark. He looked to me as though he planned to be around and running things twenty years from now himself. Then Mr. Sullivan came out on the stage and made a nice speech, asking the kids to give their respectful attention to all the very fine performers besides the Beatles who were appearing on the show, because if they didn't, he would call in a barber. The kids laughed in the kind of way that meant they thought maybe Mr. Sullivan just might call in a barber, and they calmed down. After clowning around a bit, Mr. Sullivan said, 'Our city — indeed, the country — has never seen anything like these four young men from Liverpool. Ladies and gentlemen, the Beatles!'

"When the Beatles sang 'She Loves You' and 'I Want to Hold Your Hand,' their two top tunes, it was very hard to hear them, because of the screaming. Two funny things I noticed about the screaming: (1) the kids must have known the songs cold, because they screamed louder every time the Beatles started a new verse of a song, and it wasn't always easy to tell just when that happened, and (2) the kids weren't actually looking at the Beatles themselves but at TV pictures of the Beatles that appeared on the nine or ten monitors scattered around the studio. I noticed this because the kids also began screaming louder every time a different Beatle appeared on the TV screen. The ones they screamed loudest for were Ringo, the drummer, and Paul, who was doing most of the singing because George, who *usually* does most of the singing, had laryngitis or something.

7

"Afterward, I went around backstage to the dressing rooms, where the Beatles were changing their shirts, 'I'm soaking,' said the Beatle named John. 'Got a ciggy?' John and Ringo and George left in their limousine for the Plaza, where the Beatles were staying, but Paul got left behind, so I climbed into a taxi with him and one of the public-relations men. At first, there was a taxi full of Beatle fans behind us, but it got swept away by traffic. Paul said that the Beatles had never had an audience at a rehearsal before and that it made them feel good to be playing before people instead of just into space. Then Paul said New York traffic was bad but London traffic was just as bad and Paris traffic was worse, because Frenchmen were maniac drivers. Then the public-relations man said he had lost fifty pounds, and Paul said he couldn't tell how much that was unless it was translated into stone. At the Plaza, we all got out of the taxi as quickly as possible and raced toward the elevators. Upstairs, there were a lot of policemen and hotel detectives who were whispering about how they were going to sneak the Beatles out of the hotel that evening, so they could get back to Mr. Sullivan's studio. There was nobody around except other policemen and hotel detectives, but they whispered anyway. One of them said that the Beatles were good boys, who followed the policemen's orders — not like General Eisenhower, who would listen to a detective's plan for sneaking him out of a building and then would deliberately go out another way.

"The Beatles' two concerts at Carnegie Hall were their final appearances in New York, and the events were arranged sort of like a prizefight. I had a seat on the stage, and I could see the audience, which was not quite as well behaved as the Ed Sullivan audience had been — more like the audience at a Young People's Concert of the New York Philharmonic. First, a disc jockey known as Murray the K said, 'For the one or two of you who want to leave your seats or throw things, we have people to take care of you.' Then a rather scared group of folk singers called the Briarwoods came out and fought a few preliminary rounds. Finally, the Beatles came out in gray suits with chesterfield collars and sang twelve songs, which couldn't be heard over the screaming, and Ringo almost knocked himself out jumping around, and then they bounced off the stage, looking pretty exhausted but pretty happy.

"CONCLUSIONS: The Beatles' tour of New York was a success because the Beatles are nice guys and the girls think they look cute. Also, they are worth listening to, even if they aren't as good as the Everly Brothers, which they really aren't."

Introduction to
BUILDING THE BEATLE IMAGE

An article titled "The Beatles Early Success Was Phony" appeared in the March 1972 *Music Journal* (pages 40, 55, 59–60). Penned by Joe Brinckman, a fifteen-year-old high school student, the article contends that the Beatles became a world-wide success because of a $50,000 promotion campaign by their American record label. In "Building the Beatle Image," Vance Packard explains that it took more than $50,000 worth of publicity to launch Beatlemania, outlining the five ingredients of a craze (symbol, need by audience, freshness, carrying device, and mood of the times) and illustrates how the Beatles fulfilled each one. Contrary to Packard's prediction, however, no businessman has yet been caught with a warehouse full of Beatle products.

BUILDING THE BEATLE IMAGE

by Vance Packard

What causes an international craze like the current Beatlemania?

Press agentry can only swell a craze. To get one started you need to bring into fusion five vital ingredients. This is true whether the craze involves Davy Crockett, Liberace or Elvis Presley.

Only three years ago it is doubtful that any observer of pop culture would have picked the Beatles to inspire madness on both sides of the Atlantic. In 1961 the Beatles affected a beatnik look. They wore black T-shirts, black leather jackets, blue jeans and disheveled hair. In one picture taken of them that year they scowled at the camera as good beatniks should.

Then along came Brian Epstein, an aristocratic-looking young Englishman who ran a record shop and soon became their manager. First he made them scrub, comb their hair and get into civilized clothing. Then little by little, by a combination of hunch, luck and design, he began exploiting the five ingredients that will create a craze.

First, the Beatles needed a symbol that would make them stand out in people's minds, a symbol such as the coonskin cap that Walt Disney gave to his Davy Crockett creation. For a symbol it was decided to exploit their already overlong hair. The Beatles let it grow longer and bushier, combed it forward — and then had it immaculately trimmed. The result was not only eye-catching but evocative. Such hairdos were common in the Middle Ages and the new coiffure suggested the ancient roots of England.

A second ingredient necessary for a craze is to fill some important subconscious need of teen-agers. Youngsters see themselves as a subjugated people constantly exposed to arbitrary edicts from adult authorities. The entertainment world has developed many strategies to offer youngsters a sense of escape from adult domination. Television producers of children's shows sometimes make adult figures either stupid or villainous. The press agents for some teen stars publicize the stars' defiance of their parents. Teen-age crooners relate with amiable condescension their support of their parents.

11

Rock-'n'-roll music, of course, annoys most parents, which is one of the main reasons why millions of youngsters love it. But the Beatles couldn't possibly hope to outdo Elvis Presley in appalling parents. Instead of open opposition, the Beatles practice an amiable impudence and a generalized disrespect for just about everybody. They succeeded, happily, in getting themselves denounced in some pretty high adult places. The Lord Privy Seal indicated his annoyance. And Field Marshal Lord Montgomery growled that the Army would take care of those mop-top haircuts if the Beatles were ever conscripted.

But the Beatles — under Mr. Epstein's tutelage — also have put stress on filling other subconscious needs of teen-agers. As restyled, they are no longer roughnecks but rather lovable, almost cuddly, imps. With their collarless jackets and boyish grins, they have succeeded in bringing out the mothering instinct in many adolescent girls.

The subconscious need that they fill most expertly is in taking adolescent girls clear out of this world. The youngsters in the darkened audiences can let go all inhibitions in a quite primitive sense when the Beatles cut loose. They can retreat from rationality and individuality. Mob pathology takes over, and they are momentarily freed of all of civilization's restraints.

The Beatles have become peculiarly adept at giving girls this release. Their relaxed, confident manner, their wild appearance, their whooping and jumping, their electrified rock-'n'-roll pulsing out into the darkness makes the girls want to jump — and then scream. The more susceptible soon faint or develop twitching hysteria. (One reason why Russia's totalitarian leaders frown on rock-'n'-roll and jazz is that these forms offer people release from controlled behavior.)

A third ingredient needed to get a craze started — as Brian Epstein obviously knew — is an exciting sense of freshness. In an informal poll conducted through my offspring, who are at high school and college, I find that the fact that the Beatles are somehow "different" — something new in the musical world — made the deepest impression. Teen-agers feel they are helping create something new that is peculiarly their own. And as my 15-year-old expert (feminine) explained, "We were kind of at a lag with popular singers."

The delivery, if not the music, is refreshingly different with the Beatles. Surliness is out, exuberance is in. Sloppiness is out, cleanliness is in. Self-pity is out, whooping with joy is in. Pomposity is out, humor is in.

A fourth ingredient needed to keep a craze rolling once it shows signs of starting is a carrying device, such as a theme song. The carrying device of the Beatles is found in their name. It playfully suggests beatnik, but it also suggests "beat" — and the beat is the most conspicuous feature of the Beatles' music. It is laid on heavily with both drums and bass guitar. When the screaming starts, the beat still gets through.

Finally, a craze can succeed only if it meets the mood of the times. England, after centuries of cherishing the subdued, proper form of life, is bursting out of its inhibitions. There has been a growth of open sexuality, plain speaking and living it up. The Beatles came along at just the right time to help the bursting-out process.

What is the future of the Beatle craze in America? At this point it is hard to say. But the Beatles are so dependent upon their visual appeal that there is a question whether they can sustain the craze in their American territory from across the Atlantic. Another problem is that they are not really offensive enough to grown-ups to inspire youngsters to cling to them.

Frankly, if I were in the business of manufacturing mophead Beatle wigs, I would worry. Crazes tend to die a horribly abrupt death. It was not so long ago, after all, that a good many unwary businessmen got caught with warehouses full of coonskin caps when the Crockett craze stopped almost without warning.

Introduction to
JOHN'S GOSPEL

In the beginning, John Lennon was known for making witty remarks like "women should be obscene and not heard." His comments, like his music, were bold and aggressive but still playful and harmless. As song topics grew from holding hands (*I Want to Hold Your Hand*) to one night stands (*Norwegian Wood*), John entered the realm of Controversy with his statement in the March 4, 1966, *Evening Standard* (London), concerning the relative popularity of the Beatles and Jesus Christ.

What he really said and what he really meant became clouded as the American press pounced upon the "anti-Christian" comment and reported Beatle record burnings in the South. (KLUE of Longview, Texas, held one on the day after this article appeared and was knocked off the air the very next day by a bolt of lightning.)

In the United States, the remark was defended in *The New Yorker* (August 27, 1966) and in the Jesuit magazine *America* (August 20, 1966) as a sad but true assessment of the state of Christianity. David Frost, in "John's Gospel," reviews the controversy, the first of many for John, and concludes that it revealed more about society than either the fame of the Beatles or the fate of Christianity.

JOHN'S GOSPEL

by David Frost

'The Beatles, ladies and gentlemen, the Beatles . . . . ' Mr Tommy Trinder announced to a television audience, 'They're going to have Ringo for Pope . . . They are . . . well, they've already had John and Paul . . . . '

It caused a tiny fuss, Mr Trinder must have watched amused this week as Mr John Lennon's somewhat ill-advised decision to take the analogy a stage further – linking the Beatles and Jesus – caused a rather larger furore. Or did it – *really*?

The whole incident has been an interesting little saga of press activity, of delayed-effect news-making. From the moment that John Lennon gave a splendidly bravura, splendidly-written interview to Maureen Cleave, it has been clear that one paragraph has been lying quietly, insidiously like an unexploded time-bomb, waiting for someone in search of ammunition. The fateful words were finally seized upon by *Datebook*: 'Christianity will go. It will vanish and shrink. I needn't argue about that. I am right, and I will be proved right. We're more popular than Jesus now – I don't know which will go first, rock 'n' roll or Christianity. Jesus was all right, but his disciples were thick and ordinary.'

Even the current explosion may not have been 100 per cent genuine. For the first day or two, the stories coming over the wires from New York were alarmingly general in their first paragraphs – stations were banning Beatle records, organising burning ceremonies, American teenagers were revolting, and so on – but always suspiciously vague when it came to particular examples which seemed to hinge mainly on one Mr Tommy Charles of station WAQY in Birmingham, Alabama – scarcely the barometer of the American nation: Mr Charles, who says he is thirty-six 'but I think like a teenager' or is, in other words, mentally retarded on his own admission by about twenty-one years.

This is a key problem about all stories in the British press emanating from the United States. A key problem for news editors as well as readers. It is so easy to make a trivial, untypical incident sound as if it were happening all over the American continent, and so difficult to sort out the deeper significance of three paragraphs from Washington.

It was obviously his realisation of this that made Brian Epstein get up from his sick-bed and fly over to New York to find out what on earth was going on. And yet paradoxically, by this very action, he probably gave further life to the story, which now achieved a sort of verification for the first time.

After a series of further accounts the story reached its denouement when the Beatles office in London issued a long and extraordinarily detailed apology and denial: 'Quoted and misrepresented entirely out of context. Lennon is deeply interested in religion, and was at the time having serious talks with Maureen Cleave . . . concerning religion. What he said and meant was that in the last fifty years the church in England and therefore Christ had suffered decline in interest. He did not mean to boast about the Beatles' fame. He meant to point out that the Beatles' effect appeared to be a more immediate one upon certainly the younger generation. The article was understood to be exclusive to the London *Evening Standard*. It was not anticipated that it would be displayed out of context and in such a manner as it did in an American teenage magazine.'

An interesting new concept this. All right for the London *Evening Standard*, but not for an American teenage magazine. What if it had been the American *New York Times*? or an English teenage magazine? or the London *Evening News*? And indeed what should one's attitude be to an American teenager reading the London *Evening Standard*? Anyway, the statement concludes: 'In the circumtances John is deeply concerned and regrets that people with deep religious beliefs should have been offended in any way.'

Well . . . what does one make of all that? It is not merely a question of what you think of John Lennon's original statement. You may think it was splendidly refreshing to hear a pop singer speaking his mind, whether you agreed or disagreed with what he was saying. Or you may just have thought that the Beatles were going too far and ought to be stopped by some means or other. That, however, is basically irrelevant.

First and foremost, the recantation is obviously one giant euphemism — it does not really reflect the feelings of John Lennon at the moment he made the original remark. Secondly, as Henry Thody pointed out in the *News of the World*, it does not really reflect the views of the Beatles' fans either here or in New York who all asked Thody 'Who goes to church any more except squares?' and words that were generally to that effect. Thirdly, of course, the statement does not really reflect the true feelings of our two societies — the affronted devout worshipping unanimity it seems to summon up just does not exist in the western world any more. However, as always happens when a society rightly or wrongly is laying aside the old canons and searching for new ones, the public surface maintenance of the old canons becomes even more important. It has been the same for the past few years with the Roman Catholic church and their position on birth control. The Beatles' statement has been wrung out of them by society for their failure to adhere to a code which in the main the Beatles themselves have rejected, their fans have rejected, and that self-same society has rejected.

Personally, I did not agree with much of John Lennon's statement but whatever one thinks of it and the code it attacks, should not on principle a civilised society be beyond the point where one paragraph by anyone about anything can produce this sort of hysteria?

And if, gentle reader, the events of the past week have still left you feeling bitterly that the outrageousness of people like Mr Lennon must be stopped at all costs, I would suggest, as an antidote, that you spend the next seven days reading the collected interviews of Cliff Richard.

Introduction to
THE BEATLES AND THE GURU

After a weekend with the Maharishi Mahesh Yogi in Bangor, Wales, the Beatles travelled to Rishikesh, India, in February, 1968, to meditate at the sandals of the Maharishi. The incident sparked dissension within the group (Ringo and Paul left before the end of the three month term) and criticism from outside observers. William F. Buckley comments here in "The Beatles and the Guru."

THE BEATLES AND THE GURU

by William F. Buckley

London, Feb. 28 — The doings of the Beatles are minutely recorded here in England and, as a matter of fact, elsewhere, inasmuch as it is true what one of the Beatle-gentlemen said a year or so ago, that they are more popular than Jesus Christ. It is a matter of considerable public interest that all four of the Beatles have gone off to a place called Rishikesh, in India, to commune with one Maharishi Mahesh Yogi.

The gentleman comes from India, and the reigning chic stipulates that Mysterious India is where one goes to Have a Spiritual Experience. Accordingly, the Beatles are there, as also Mia Farrow, who, having left Frank Sinatra, is understandably in need of spiritual therapy; and assorted other types. It isn't altogether clear what is the drill at Rishikesh, except that — and this visibly disturbed a couple of business managers of the Beatles — a postulant at the shrine of Mr. Yogi is expected to contribute a week's salary as an initiation fee. A week's salary may not be very much for thee and me, but it is a whole lot of sterling for a Beatle, and one gathers from the press that the business managers thought this a bit much, and rather wish that the Beatles could find their spiritual experience a little less dearly.

The wisdom of Maharishi Mahesh Yogi is not rendered in easily communicable tender. It is recorded by one disciple that he aroused himself from a trance sufficiently to divulge the sunburst, "Ours is an age of science, not faith," a seizure of spiritual exertion which apparently left him speechless with exhaustion, I mean, wouldn't you be exhausted if you came up with that? It is reported that the Beatles were especially transfigured when the Maharishi divulged, solemnly, that "speech is just the progression of thought." One can assume that the apogee of their experience was reached upon learning, from the guru's own mouth, that "anything that comes from direct experience can be called science."

I am not broke, but I think that if I were, I would repair to India, haul up a guru's flag and — I guarantee it — I would be the most

23

successful guru of modern times. I would take the Beatles' weekly salary, and Mia Farrow's, and the lot of them, and I would come up with things like: "Put on therefore, as the elect of God, holy and beloved, bowels of mercies, kindness, humbleness of mind, meekness, longsuffering; forbearing one another, and forgiving one another, if any man have a quarrel against any; even as *** forgave you, so also do ye. And above all these things put on charity, which is the bond of perfectness. And let the peace of God rule in your hearts, to the which also ye are called in one body; and be thankful."

Can it be imagined that I would be less successful, quoting these lines, from a single letter of St. Paul, than Maharishi Mahesh Yogi has been? The truly extraordinary feature of our time isn't the faithlessness of the Western people, it is their utter, total ignorance of the Christian religion. They travel to Rishikesh to listen to pallid seventh-hand imitations of thoughts and words they never knew existed. They will go anywhere to experience spirituality — except next door. An Englishman need go no further than to hear Evensong at King's College at Oxford, or to hear high Mass at Chartres Cathedral; or to read St. Paul, or John, or the psalmists. Read a volume by Chesterton — *The Everlasting Man; Orthodoxy; The Dumb Ox;* and the spiritual juices begin to run, but no, Christianity is, well, well what? Well, unknown. The Beatles know more about carburetors than they know about Christianity, which is why they, like so many others, make such asses of themselves in pursuit of Mr. Gaga Yogi. Their impulse is correct, and they reaffirm, as man always has, and always will, the truism that man is a religious animal. If only they knew what is waiting there, available to them, right there in Jollie Olde Englande, no costlier than 2/6d at the local bookstore. It is too easy nowadays to found new religions, though the vogue is constant. Voltaire was once abashed at the inordinate iconoclasm of one of his young disciples who asked the Master how might he go about founding a new religion. "Well," Voltaire said, "begin by getting yourself killed. Then rise again on the third day."

(Washington Star Syndicate, Inc.)

Introduction to
THE CURIOUS CASE OF THE "DEATH"
OF PAUL McCARTNEY

The imagined death of a Beatle only months before the announced breakup of the band is viewed from a sociological perspective by Barbara Suczek in "The Curious Case of the 'Death' of Paul McCartney." Suczek reviews several "clues" found on album covers and in songs and explains the strange phenomenon as a quasi-religious experience for a legion of devoted believers.

THE CURIOUS CASE OF THE "DEATH"
OF PAUL McCARTNEY

by Barbara Suczek

It is a widely held notion that we are a disillusioned people living in a disenchanted age. Indeed, a belief that scientific advance inevitably leads to the demystification of the world — an eventuality that is sometimes celebrated and sometimes deplored is so prevalent that it is virtually a modern axiom.

But to interpret *mystery* so passively to think of it as being merely the effect of ignorance is to neglect the implications of the active verb form: to mystify. Mystification does not, exclusively, *happen*; it can also be enacted. To mystify and to demystify are valid alternatives which humans can, if they choose, use in the pursuit of their individual or collective purposes.

An interesting example of the social construction of a mystery occurred in the late months of 1969, when a strange surge of excitement spread across the country, fomented, apparently, by persistent rumors relating to the nature and circumstances of the alleged death of Beatle Paul McCartney. By the end of October, the major news media were actively engaged in reporting the phenomenon.

Thus, a dispatch from Detroit appearing in the *San Francisco Chronicle* (October 23) stated, "The news editor of radio station WKNR, which has been researching rumors and speculations about McCartney's death, said McCartney called to dispel rumors he might be dead."

The *New York Times* (November 2) said, "The half-belief in the rumor reached such proportions that WMCA's Alec Bennett was sent to London to see if he could unearth some facts which might prove or dispel the stories. 'The only way McCartney is going to quell the rumors,' Bennett said, 'is by coming up with a set of fingerprints from a 1965 passport which can be compared to his present prints.' " *Life* (November 7) carried a statement from McCartney himself, in

---

which he suggested, "Perhaps the rumor started because I haven't been much in the press lately."

Certainly the story had a strange quality about it: it seemed ghostly in sort as well as in content — the rumor of a rumor. Even the original was obscure, tending itself to drift into rumor.

The most consistent account of its genesis pointed to an account in a college paper. The *New York Times* (November 2), in an article substantially agreeing with a similar report in the *San Francisco Chronicle* (October 22), said:

> This fantastic death wish seems to have been stimulated by a University of Michigan undergraduate named Fred LaBour . . . in which he expounded at length on the elaborate clues indicating that McCartney had died and been replaced by a stand-in . . . . Actually the story seems to have originated in the Midwest when a trio of disc jockeys on WKNR-FM in Detroit decided that a slew of purely symbolic clues on various Beatles' record jackets and in the lyrics of songs meant that the Beatles had pulled off the most stupendous and elaborate hoax in the history of the world.

The *Rolling Stone* (November 15) did not agree that the story had originated in Michigan:

> LaBour . . . has turned out the most baroque explication of Paul's supposed death (though he was not the first to get it in print: the Northern Star student paper at Illinois University carried an article headlined, "Clues Hint at Possible Beatle Death" on September 23, almost a month earlier.)

Whatever its source, the story spread widely and persistently. In New York, it was reported that "thousands of fans kept vigil at their radios" and that "mourners began appearing outside the McCartney home in London." The *San Francisco Chronicle* claimed that radio stations and newspapers were being deluged with calls asking, "Is Paul dead?"[1] Beatle publicist Derek Taylor was quoted late in November as saying that his Los Angeles office had received "letters and phone calls, day and night, nonstop since mid-October." A professor at the University of Miami reportedly "applied scientific voice detector tests to some Beatle records and concluded that three different voices are attributed to Paul McCartney." *Life* carried "The Case of the 'Missing' Beatle" as its cover story for November 7, presumably thus bringing the rumor to the attention of the remote outposts of the literate world.

The story, in gist, is as follows: Paul McCartney was allegedly killed in an automobile accident in England in November 1966. The remaining Beatles, fearing that public reaction to the news would adversely affect the fortunes of the group, agreed among themselves to keep the matter a secret. Since it was obvious that Paul could not

28

simply disappear from their midst without rousing a storm of embarrassing questions, they hit upon the idea of hiring a double to play his part in public,[2] a role that was filled to perfection by the winner of a Paul McCartney Look-Alike Contest, an orphan from Edinburgh named William Campbell. By an astonishing stroke of good luck, it turned out that Campbell not only bore a striking physical resemblance to McCartney, but was also endowed with similar musical abilities so that, with a bit of practice, he was able to sustain a performance that completely deceived an attentive and discriminating audience for almost three years. A slight awkwardness developed when a private affair intruded upon the public image: "Campbell" married the lady of his own choice, Linda Eastman, causing a short-lived flurry of consternation among Beatle fans who had for some time been expecting Paul to marry British actress Jane Asher. Miss Asher, the story goes, was paid a handsome sum to be quiet.

For some unspecified reason, however, and at some unspecified time, the plot seems to have undergone a qualitative change. "What began," according to the *Berkeley Tribe* (October 14–30), "for John Lennon as a scheme of deception conceived during moments of personal shock — and perhaps despair — developed into an all-encompassing religious vision."

Lennon's "all-encompassing religious vision," we are asked to believe, was oddly manifested by inserting cryptic messages relating to McCartney's death into the lyrics of songs and among the decorations on the Beatles' album covers.

The catalog of "buried" clues is lengthy and ingenious.[3] It includes such observations as the following: on the cover of *Magical Mystery Tour*, three Beatles are pictured wearing red carnations: McCartney's is black. On the centerfold of *Sgt. Pepper's Band*, McCartney is wearing an arm patch reading "O.P.D." which assertedly stands for "Officially Pronounced Dead" and is the British equivalent of "DOA" (Dead On Arrival). In "I Am the Walrus," McCartney (or his reasonably accurate facsimile) sings, "I am he as you are me and I am the walrus."* The significance of this line is that "walrus" is supposed to be the Greek word for "corpse" — etymological authority not cited. (Webster says, "walrus" is Scandinavian in origin.) If the song "Revolution No. 9" is played backwards, a voice (whose?) seems to say, "Turn me on, dead man!"

It is undoubtedly difficult for anyone not immediately caught up in the collective excitement generated by this macabre story to take seriously the symbols regarded as significant by those who were intensely involved in it. Nevertheless, for a period of several weeks[4]

---

*Editor's note: John Lennon sings "I Am the Walrus," not Paul McCartney.

they *were* taken seriously and by a surprisingly diverse body of people.

Active rumor participants fell, basically, into three groups or publics: *believers*, who accepted the story at its face value; *skeptics*, who suspected it was a publicity plant to stimulate record sales; and *unbelievers*, who were convinced that the phenomenon was a manifestation of psychosocial pathology. Age was the most obvious variable separating the believers from the other two groups, believers being usually in the adolescent age range from about twelve to twenty. Older participants frequently seemed embarrassed by their own interest, tending to deprecate it even when the animation of their discussion seemed to belie the disclaimers.

Between and among the publics there developed considerable antagonism. It should be emphasized that, regardless of their credulity stance, all these groups were actively contributing to the rumor process — the very act of opposition, irrespective of its direction, seeming to inflame tempers and produce rhetorical rejoinders. Rather than working together dialectically to create a consensual explanation for new and ambiguous events (a functional process theoretically attributed to rumor; Shibutani, 1966: 183), the publics in this instance seemed to withdraw into fixed camps, facing each other as factional forces dedicated to the defense of separate positions.

On the surface of it, it would seem reasonable to suppose that both the rumor and the factionalism centering around it might readily have been dispelled by the introduction of objective, reliable evidence confirming or disconfirming the fact of McCartney's death. The effect of the flow of information provided by the mass media, however, proved to be singularly unsuccessful in reducing public tension. Regardless of the play of coverage: "verified" facts, statements from McCartney, photographs of McCartney making the statements — the effect was to add fuel to the fire.

The stickler, apparently, is the matter of credulity: what evidence will be accepted as *reliable* evidence and by whom is not necessarily decided simply and objectively. Certainly the believers in the death story felt no lack of evidence in support of their belief. *Evidence* was the whole point! They were fortified, bulwarked, armed to the teeth with evidence: they had a veritable overkill of evidence.

The fact of the matter was that each public would accept as credible evidence only such data as suited the logic of its own cognitive system and thus it was that the more McCartney's death was denied, including by himself, the more the tension and hostility seemed to increase, feeding in and out of the interfactional dispute.

To account for the initial appearance of the rumor is, perhaps, the most perplexing aspect of the phenomenon. It seemed to emerge from out of nowhere, in response to nothing in particular and, as if at once to explain and justify its presence, the clues seemed similarly to emerge. But to realize the fact of the death depended upon recognizing the existence of the clues, and the clues were only recognizable if one were aware of the death. And so there is no external logic to guide a decision as to where the fundamental ambiguity lies — in the death or in the clues — since it is impossible to establish a priority between them.

It *is* possible, retrospectively, to note changes in the behavior of the Beatles that may have contributed to public curiosity and speculation of the sort which — according to rationalistic, demystifying theories of rumor function — rumor is frequently addressed.

(1) Due to the increasing complexity of their music, requiring the use of elaborate technical equipment and the manpower to manipulate it, the Beatles had reportedly been experiencing difficulty in presenting concerts that would satisfy the rising expectations of their record-listening public and, at the same time, uphold their image as a self-reliant, spontaneous group of four. For this reason, apparently, the number of their personal appearances had been decreasing.

(2) There were indications that the Beatles, as individuals, were growing weary of the limelight and developing correspondingly a taste for privacy and seclusion with the effect that, as in the previous case, they were becoming less visible to their fans.

(3) Paul McCartney had had a falling out with the other members of the group as the result of a dispute over management, as a consequence of which he had withdrawn from a number of Beatles' activities.

(4) McCartney had taken his fans by surprise by marrying Linda Eastman rather than, as had long been predicted, Jane Asher.

While these occurrences may very well have raised some questions among ardent Beatle fans, in and of themselves they do not appear to be sufficiently inexplicable or momentous to account for the fantastic content and public scope of the death rumor.

Clearly, the rumor's underlying logic is difficult to discern — so difficult, in fact, that — if logic can be said to exist at all — it appears that it must be sought outside the immediate subject of discourse. If this is the case, the rumor should be regarded as essentially symbolic, its characters and events standing for as yet unknown (and perhaps unknowable) social concerns. As such, its function is symptomatic; expressive rather than expository, problem-indicative rather than problem-solving.

The intriguing question inevitably poses itself as to why a group of young English pop singers should become the symbol for the expression of a social malaise. A clear answer is not easy to provide. It does seem reasonable to assume, however, that it is in some way related to the climate of intense excitement the group universally seemed to evoke.

The Beatles captured the public imagination almost from the beginning. Hunter Davies (1968: 179) says:

> Beatlemania descended on the British Isles in October, 1963, just as the Christine Keeler--Profumo scandal fizzed out. It didn't lift for three years, by which time it had spread and had covered the whole world . . . . It is impossible to exaggerate Beatlemania because Beatlemania was in itself an exaggeration . . . . It wasn't just teenagers: people of all ages and intellects had succumbed, though perhaps not all as hysterically as the teenagers.

Time (August 12, 1966) quoted John Lennon as saying that the Beatles were more popular than Jesus, an observation that occasioned cries of outrage but which may, for all that, have contained a grain of truth.[5]

The astonishing popularity of the group was probably due to a combination of factors, among them being the personal charm and youth of its principals, their exciting new music, and the phenomenon of mass communication. (The hysteria was unquestionably nurtured by publicity-conscious entrepreneurs.) When these elements came into contact with the Baby Boom generation — the largest group in the history of the world whose members were simultaneously in the period of adolescent identity differentiation — the effect was electric, in more ways than one.

Parents, educators, and clergymen viewed the phenomenon with alarm: the shaggy Beatle hairstyle looked bizarre to them and seemed to presage the ultimate collapse of middle-class values. The music sounded, if anything, more ominous than the hair looked, and the noise level achieved by the electronic instruments was predicted by "experts" to be a potential source of hearing loss and possible deafness. The, to say the least, *immoderate* behavior of some of the youthful fans in the presence of their idols was much publicized and completely unsettling to their elders. The John Birch Society was reported to regard the Beatles as part of an international Communist plot to demoralize American youth.

The more the older generation imprecated, the more cohesive in their devotion to the Beatles the youngsters seemed to become.

This is not intended to suggest that it was necessarily characteristic of adults to oppose the Beatles. On the contrary, there were many adults who were enthusiastic Beatle fans. There was, however, a marked tendency among adults — quite apart from whatever credulity stance they might individually assume in regard to the death rumor — to split into factions marked by opposing social and political values. Conservatives, for example, were much more likely to be negatively disposed toward the Beatles than were liberals.

It would be obviously absurd to argue that the Beatles — even had they been motivated to do so — could have produced this strange ferment of age partisanship cross-cut by political partisanship. Such a notion would surely exceed the fondest fantasy of the most ambitious public relations engineer! If the Beatles became the vehicle for the expression of preexisting social divisions (as they apparently did), it is probably due to a series of historical coincidences, not the least of which being the same sort of interesting propinquity that moved Hilary to climb Everest: they were conspicuously and invitingly *there*!

The most striking characteristic of the McCartney phenomenon is probably its preoccupation with the covert. Whether emphasizing *concealment* — as in the idea that the rumor was covering a sales promotional gimmick — or *revelation* — that it stemmed from John Lennon's motivation to communicate "the truth" — the "hidden meaning" motif recurs thematically both in the content of the rumor and in the explanations put forth to account for it.

There are, in all likelihood, many and various reasons for a public fascination with the idea of the concealed. The death rumor may be, for example, an inconsequential but interesting expression of the ethos of the Freudian epoch: an essentially artistic creation indicating public awareness of the concept of the unconscious — a folk equivalent of Surrealism.

Again, the fact that many persons apparently resisted all reasonable explications offered in the mass media, preferring to accept interpretations stressing occultism and deceit, may point to a widespread lack of faith in the reliability of information received through formal channels of communication. It may indicate that the much-discussed "credibility gap" is taking its toll by developing publics increasingly inclined to turn to folk communicational resources.[6]

However, the strange content of the rumor and its obdurate quality — the previously discussed failure of its publics to interest themselves in reaching consensual explanation — both suggest that there is something more than a mistrust of news agencies involved in this instance.

Another possibility is that there is demonstrated here a process of ordering seemingly random and chaotic facts into a system of meaning, the sense of the covert being somehow related to an inherent significance which is assumed to *underlie* the events of the world.

The Beatles had, over the years, moved from the straightforward, comprehensible statements of the "I Want to Hold Your Hand" —

"I Saw Her Standing There" period of 1963 to the confusing and seemingly unintegrated verbal streams that are characteristic of many of the 1967 songs: "Lucy in the Sky with Diamonds," for example, and "I Am the Walrus."

The "absurdity" of the songs was reflected in the style of the album cover decorations, those of the later years being typically designed as collages of apparently unrelated and randomly selected items.

Randomness can create a fertile field for subjective interpretation: one man's nonsense is another's apocalypse. To avoid the terror stemming from idiosyncratic isolation, however, it is necessary to establish a social basis of confirmation — some criterial standard — that what one takes to be a meaning is accepted and shared by others. Some such meaning-establishing process seemed to be indicated by the behavior of the younger adolescents as they busily conferred with one another evaluating the orthodoxy of the existence and interpretation of specific "clues."

It may be that the McCartney rumor reflects a search for meaning that runs much deeper than a seemingly frivolous preoccupation with pop song lyrics and album cover art would seem to suggest. In periods of social unrest and upheaval, when traditional sources of authority are being challenged and overthrown, there is always the danger that human institutions will dissolve into primal meaninglessness. We may, in our own society, be presently witnessing the proliferation of interest in such occult phenomena as the *I-Ching*, astrology, Eastern mysticism, drug revelations, and the like, manifestations of efforts to shore up crumbling meaning systems. Perhaps there is a search for a new basis of authority and understanding represented here that is as profound as, on the surface, it may appear ridiculous.

That this fascination with the mystic seems particularly prevalent among the young makes sense when explained in the theoretical terms of adolescent identity crisis. Since it is this age group that most typically lacks the integrated convictions that might help to sustain a sense of basic meaning in times of extreme and rapid change, these are logically the ones whose worlds are most vulnerable when established bases of authority are assaulted.

In the past, it has surely been the function of great religions to organize and sustain the meanings and values of a society, but ours is a secular age. Basic religious tenets have been increasingly challenged by science; basic religious values have been subordinated to marketplace competition. It is probably not strange, then, that many aspects of the McCartney death story suggest an abortive attempt to apotheosize Paul McCartney.[8]

There are five specific properties of the McCartney phenomenon that would seem to support a conjecture that a myth- or legend-creating process was at work.

(1) The content was relatively stable,[9] lacking the ongoing, developmental quality that usually characterizes a news story. Among its believers, the story was taught and learned, deviations from the theme were definitively discouraged, and the fundamental details were memorized like a litany.

(2) The story shared with the legend a quality of empirical irrelevance. To whom, after all, but a few academicians, does it matter if legendary heroes actually lived and did the deeds attributed to them? The significance of the story transcends the details of individual biography. The fact, or lack of it, of the death of Paul McCartney seemed similarly irrelevant to its publics. The inference, then, is that the Paul McCartney of this story was a symbol, a social construct that no longer required the facts of a personal existence to sustain it.

(3) An almost Gothic engrossment with death and the occult permeated virtually every aspect of the phenomenon — twin themes that are fundamental to myth.[10]

(The above properties, taken together, seem to fall into a familiar and ancient pattern. One senses in their conjunction a curious mandate that something must be fulfilled, calling for the recapitulation of a legend.)

(4) The content of the story recalls the pattern that categorically defines a cyclical myth. The untimely death of a beautiful youth who is subsequently transformed into or revealed to be a god is a recurrent mythical theme and is presumed to reflect the cyclical process in nature. The legends of Osiris, Adonis, Dionysis, and Jesus have all conformed, in some major way, to this pattern. It may be that the McCartney rumor represents an aborted attempt to re-create such a myth. Perhaps in the present, as in the past, humans may be trying to make sense out of the apparent senselessness of their own deaths by suggesting, analogously, the possibility of reincarnation. Alternatively. such a myth may be a process whereby socially valued qualities of an exemplary youth can be abstracted into an idealized model and thus preserved from the eroding onslaughts of ongoing reality (a motivation described by Wallace Stevens as "nostalgia for perfection.")

Whatever the reason for the recurring beautiful-dead-youth theme, its resonance in the McCartney story was clearly discernible. An embarrassed but eerie longing for the story to be true — for Paul to be really dead — was repeatedly expressed, such expression being invariably accompanied by protestations of admiration or love for the singer.

(5) Clearly the rumor had high entertainment value. Not only did it provide a fascinating subject for conversation, but it also invoked — particularly among younger adolescents — a fearful, brooding, supernatural mood which they obviously found rather more enjoyable than otherwise.[11] The entertainment component is an important factor in the promulgation of a myth since the pleasure of its company makes its repetition a likelihood.[12]

While there is a tendency to assume that myths and legends are essentially relics left to us, more or less by accident, from a long-departed and unenlightened age, there are many indications that the myth-making process is socially vigorous in the modern era. The spectacular rise of Mormonism in the nineteenth century is a striking example both of latter-day myth-making and the organizing force for social action that can emanate from a sacred mystery (and the myth that symbolizes it). Mystery resulting from ignorance can pose a potential and serious threat to human survival; as such, it urges the pursuit of knowledge to dispel it. Mystery, on the other hand, can provide a basis for human meaning, its sacred (and secret) premises upholding the perception of reality. In its latter function, it can be created and preserved by social volition; it can be institutionalized into a religion.

There are several factors that might help to explain why Paul McCartney may have become the unwitting subject of a religious myth. In the first place, there is the underlying context of the ecstatic reaction, especially among the young, elicited by the Beatles and their music. There can be little doubt that rock groups produce an auditory, visual, and sexual stimulation that is particularly impelling because of the intense effects made possible by electronics — sound patterns heretofore impossible to produce and control, mind-splitting amplification. Heightened psychophysical reactions thus induced are further augmented by the contagion of collective excitement sweeping through vast audiences — the very size of the audience having been itself made possible by electrically amplified sound.

Since religion and ecstatic reaction have never been far apart, such orgiastic response might very easily be transferred into religious ecstasy. Middle-class nervousness in the face of religious intensity is quite accountable among people for whom rationality in the social order is particularly valued. These are rarely the young and even more rarely, evidently, the contemporary American young. The irrationality of ecstatic response may be the factor that can best explain the previously noted antagonism expressed by conservative adults not only to the rumor but to the entire Beatlemania phenomenon.

The precipitating agent transforming collective excitement into religious response might, hypothetically, have been a fortuitous juxtaposition of ideas. There are always disconnected and intriguing bits of commonly available information floating about in segments of society without an organizing explanation to pull them together: data in search of a theory. Relevant to the McCartney case such items might range from the high drama of the deaths of the Kennedy brothers — never explained wholly to the satisfaction of the general public — through the rumor-productive, year-long hiatus of Bob Dylan following a serious motorcycle accident; the accidental death of singer Richard Farina just as his career was gaining momentum; a curious public awareness of the rarely discussed death of one of the original members of the Beatles; the group's venture into Indian mysticism in 1967; John Lennon's previously mentioned comment, irrevocably, perhaps, linking together the idea of the Beatles and Jesus.

The choice of McCartney as a specific focus of attention may rest on the situational ambiguities mentioned above in which he, probably because of the vagaries of personal temperament, seems to have been a key figure. Added to this is the apparently undeniable fact that McCartney was regarded by many as the most handsome and the most romantically appealing of the Beatles. This being the case, it seems quite probable that Paul would be the most likely member of the group to be cast in the role of ritual sacrificial victim. He might very well have been, for a month or so, a candidate for deification — saved this embarrassment in the end not so much by his own stubborn insistence on proclaiming himself to be alive as by the approach of the Christmas holidays. There, in a strange sort of way, but for the grace of God, went God.

The public stir attending the "death" of Paul McCartney was obviously an amusing but trivial social phenomenon: short-lived and probably inconsequential. That it should have spread as widely and as rapidly as it did, however, suggests that there are processes of social interaction at work that it might well behoove us to examine more carefully. However foolish its guise, the McCartney rumor clearly indicates that there is a potential for irrational belief and action — be it constructive or be it destructive to what or whose values — that is alive and well in the modern, industrialed, "enlightened" world.

NOTES

1. A similar phenomenon was noted in the wake of the death of Franklin Roosevelt: "newspapers, radio stations, banks, and even corner drugstores were deluged with calls asking if it 'was true' that this that or the other person had died or been killed in an accident" (Jacobson, 1948: 460). The "secretly dead" pattern has its "secretly alive" counterpart. Thus, according to Jacobson (1948),

Roosevelt "quite apparently died as a man dies from a cerebral hemorrhage. But, according to the echoes of rumor, Roosevelt is still alive, in a madhouse."

In the past few years, there has been a recurrent rumor that John F. Kennedy did not die in Dallas but that he is being concealed — disfigured and brain-damaged — in a military hospital "somewhere" in the United States.

2.   The "double" theme is a recurring one. During World War II, it was circulated in the United States relative to Adolf Hitler. Recently, we have heard it asserted of Mao Tse-tung. Jacobson (1948) mentions it in connection with Napoleon Bonaparte.

3.   From the *Rolling Stone* (January 7, 1971): "*Interviewer:* Were any of those things really on the albums that were said to be there? The clues? *John Lennon:* No. That was bullshit, the whole thing was made up . . . . We did put in like 'tit, tit, tit' in 'Girl.' "

4.   On the basis of a quick rundown of press reports, it can be roughly estimated that the period of intense public excitement, at least the period during which the news media were actively contributing to it, lasted for approximately two months, reaching a peak in early November. After the last week in November, interest seemed to peter out, the most likely explanation being that public interest had been diverted by the approach of the holiday season. There was a brief afterglow on February 23, 1970, in a TV skit on Rowan and Martin's *Laugh-In: "Angel I:* Is there any truth to the rumor that Paul McCartney is still alive? *Angel II:* I doubt it. Where do you think we get these groovy harp arrangements?"

5.   For example, the following is from an interview with a fourteen-year-old high school freshman (male) in November 1969: "Well, I hate to say it, but Jesus doesn't turn me on like the Beatles do. I feel like a hypocrite, but I think John Lennon was right when he said that. I get turned on by our church group, though. Like when we sit around together and discuss Galatians and we're all together and you really turn on. Like you love everybody — feel close to everybody. . . . The Beatles are good. They tell the truth. They believe in love and people. They're against hypocrisy. They turn you on!"

6.   And, as Leonard Schatzman has pointed out to me, the reverse can also hold true: folk communicational processes can create their own credibility gap.

7.   Davies (1968: 282) notes: "They have used drug slang in their songs, but not as much as people have said . . . . They are amused by all the interpretations. John deliberately let all the verbal jokes and stream-of-consciousness stuff stay as they had come out of his head in "I Am the Walrus," knowing a lot of people would have fun trying to analyze them."

John Lennon (*Rolling Stone*, February 4, 1971) says: " 'Lucy in the Sky with Diamonds' — I swear to God, or Mao, or to anybody you like, I had no idea spelled L.S.D. — I didn't look at the initials, I don't look — I mean, I never play things backwards."

8.   The inherent religiosity of the rumor has been noted by a number of writers. For example: J. Marks (*New York Times*, November 2, 1969): "The death and resurrection of heroes appears to be as important to the generation that worships rock as it is to the tribes that celebrate the demise and return of various vegetable gods. Whether the McCartney death is purely physical or metaphorical or even metaphysical, it is probable that there is more than a little of the mythic logic of the Cambridge school of classical anthropology involved

in the Paul-Messiah myth."

Ralph J. Gleason (*San Francisco Examiner*, November 5, 1969): "They've got it all wrong. It's God that's dead, not Paul McCartney . . . . No one believes in anything any more and man has a deep need to believe. Remove his objects of belief and he will invent others."

John Lennon (*Rolling Stone*, January 7, 1971): "Whenever we were on tour in Britain and everywhere we went, there were always a few seats laid aside for cripples and people in wheelchairs . . . the mothers would push them at you like you were Christ or something, or as if there were some aura about you which would rub off on them . . . . It seemed like we were just surrounded by cripples and blind people all the time, and when we would go through corridors, they would all be touching us and things like that. It was horrifying."

9. "Legends persist because . . . they provide answers to the persistent riddles of life or, with fine or only metaphoric precision, deep human feelings . . . . Legends that deal with primal forces, cosmology, religious belief, are technically called *myths* . . . they are especially resistant to change" (Allport and Postman, 1967: 164).

10. "The roots of myth and ritual [go] down to the black subsoil of the grave-cult and the fear of death" (Max Muller in Campbell, 1969: 31).

11. Typical comments of thirteen- and fourteen-year olds are the following: "It makes me all tingly!" " . . . dark! It's a very *dark* feeling. I don't know how else to tell you." "It's mysterious and creepy. Sometimes it's depressing." "You're hooked in to something — something strange!"

12. "[Myths] are religious recitations conceived as symbolic of the play of eternity in time . . . . Myths and legends may furnish entertainment incidentally, but they are essentially tutorial" (Campbell, 1969: 16).

REFERENCES

ALLPORT, G.V. and L. POSTMAN (1967) The Psychology of Rumor. New York: Henry Holt.
CAMPBELL, J. (1969) The Flight of the Wild Gander. New York: Viking.
DAVIES, H. (1968) The Beatles: The Authorized Biography. New York: Mc-Graw-Hill.
JACOBSON, D.J. (1948) The Affairs of Dame Rumor. New York: Rinehart.
SHIBUTANI, T. (1966) Improvised News. Indianapolis, Ind.: Bobbs-Merrill.

FURTHER READING
PART I

If you have been wondering why there is no book telling what the Beatles did on every single day of their lives — wonder no longer! The book is *The Beatles, A Day in the Life* (Pierian Press, 1980; Quick Fox, 1981), by Tom Schultheiss. It may not account for every day of their lives, but it details quite a few between 1960 and 1970. Author Schultheiss compiled the dates from over fifty publications, and indicates inaccuracies and conflicting sources.

Late in their collective career the Beatles made some very outspoken and controversial remarks (John's line about Jesus, Paul's admission that he used LSD), but few early interviews with the American press were as candid as the one they granted to Jean Shepherd for *Playboy* (February 1965, pages 51–60). The interview was conducted in October, 1964, and the group talks honestly about rude fans, the press and their confused religious convictions. The piece starts with the customary Beatle banter, but eventually they drop their defenses and admit that some of the cute quips heard at press conferences were actually ghost-written by press agent Derek Taylor. Toward the end, John speculates that the interview will appear short in print after the editors omit words like " 'crap' and 'bloody' and 'tit' and 'bastard.' " A reverent thought for the irreverent John, but the words were not omitted.

Derek Taylor, the man who whispered in their ears at some of those early press conferences, tells his story as press agent to the Beatles in *As Time Goes By* (Straight Arrow Books, 1973; Pierian Press, 1983). In his hip adman prose, Taylor tells of leaving the Beatle organization in the middle 1960s to work for famous American entertainers and finally to return to London to witness the decay of Apple Corps Ltd. Fellow traveller and employee of Taylor's, Richard DiLello, the Apple "house hippie," adds to the total of insider books with *The Longest Cocktail Party* (Playboy Press, 1972; Pierian Press, 1983). The Beatles themselves are distant in DiLello's book; he describes instead the chaos of the Apple office from September, 1968, to mid-1971.

41

"The unmaking of the Beatles" is chronicled almost from the start of their career in *Apple to the Core* (Pocket Books, 1972) by Peter McCabe and Robert D. Schonfeld. McCabe and Schonfeld cite the death of manager Brian Epstein as the single most important event contributing to the demise of the Beatles' creative and financial partnerships.

Ron Schaumberg, in his worm's-eye view *Growing Up with the Beatles* (Pyramid Books, 1976; Perigee Books, 1980), offers a fan's account of the Paul McCartney death hoax and a list of clues. No list of clues is really complete, and he misses two clinchers: (1) the backward mumbling between *I'm So Tired* and *Blackbird*, on the LP **The Beatles**, is really John saying "Paul is dead man, miss him, miss him, miss him," and (2) if you hold a small, frameless mirror along the length of and perpendicular to the word "HEARTS" on the cover of the LP **Sergeant Pepper's Lonely Hearts Club Band**, it reads "HE (a diamond shape with its top point indicating Paul) DIE." It may sound like a tale of the bizarre and unusual, but some devotees are still looking for clues.

Part II
Three Albums

Introduction to
"RUBBER SOUL" AND
THE SOCIAL DANCE TRADITION

Terence J. O'Grady received a Ph.D. in music from the University of Wisconsin-Madison in 1975; his dissertation, *The Music of the Beatles from 1962 to "Sergeant Pepper's Lonely Hearts Club Band*," makes rewarding (but challenging) reading for the advanced Beatles reader. In this essay, based on his dissertation, O'Grady examines the American version of the LP **Rubber Soul** as the group's boldest musical statement. (The American release is differentiated from the British release by the omission of the songs *Drive My Car, What Goes On* and *If I Needed Someone*, all to be saved for the American LP **Yesterday and Today**, and the addition of *I've Just Seen a Face* and *It's Only Love* from the British LP **Help!**.) By denying the dance-oriented conventions of commercial rock-and-roll, O'Grady argues, the Beatles achieve a "subtle triumph" with **Rubber Soul**, and contributed to the expanding definition of the pop music idiom.

"RUBBER SOUL" AND
THE SOCIAL DANCE TRADITION

by Terence J. O'Grady

By the end of 1965, the Beatles had established themselves as successful hit-makers in both an up-tempo pop-rock style and a moderate or slow tempo ballad style.[1] The first of these had been influenced by a number of different precursors — Buddy Holly, the Everlys, Chuck Berry, and a number of black motown singers — but had coalesced by 1964 into an original combination of inventive melodic and harmonic gestures and compelling, if occasionally simplistic, lyrics. Their ballad style had drawn from the standard fifties' white ballad style of Holly and others as well as the more tension-filled black style, while demonstrating glimpses of a sophisticated adult commercial style.

The British version of the *Help!* album (released in August, 1965) showed a further development of the pop-rock style, along with the finest examples of the adult commercial style to date — "Yesterday." However, two of its songs, "I've Just Seen A Face," and "It's Only Love," are found also on the American version of the *Rubber Soul* album and at least one of these seems to belong more rightfully to that album on the basis of style.

Wilfrid Mellers has stated that the title, *Rubber Soul*, "hints at greater flexibilities of irony and compassion" (1973: 58).[2] While perhaps this literary rather than any musical idea most completely binds together all of the songs on both versions of the album, the use of the word "soul" clearly has no specifically musical implications insofar as any reference to the popular black rhythm and blues of the period is intended. In terms of the influence of black music, probably no Beatle album has as little "soul" as this one.

Although the album title appears to have little musical significance, the album cover may provide a hint as to the Beatles' musical intent. The four Beatles are pictured in decidedly "rustic" attire — a far cry from the conservative "mod" fashions displayed on earlier covers. This folk-like western image is reflected in the music to some degree by the limited use of the electric guitar and, more significantly, by the general lack of broad, ear-catching pop-rock musical gestures.

McCartney's "I've Just Seen A Face" begins the album and is generally representative of *Rubber Soul* in style and approach. The recording makes use exclusively of acoustic guitars — one twelve-string guitar and two folk guitars. After a half-speed introduction featuring the folk guitars in melodic thirds, the tempo quickens to an undanceable speed and McCartney's tight, country-flavored vocal enters with a melody distinguished only by its typically Beatle-style use of accented nonharmonic tones over the stereotyped I-vi-IV-V chord progression. The country-western aura is confirmed by the added vocal harmony in the chorus.[3] Lennon adds his equally flat-toned voice in a duet of thirds and fifths over an even more basic harmonic progression.

Since the instrumental accompaniment is equally devoid of any specific rock and roll gesture (the twelve-string solo approximates Bluegrass style in rhythmic regularity, and the dull percussion off-beats fail to contribute much energy), the overall result is the Beatles' first authentically country-western (as opposed to country-rock or rockabilly) song — a genre not normally considered palatable to the popular market of 1965 by the recording industry. (The other song released earlier on the British *Help!* album, "It's Only Love," occupies a more ambiguous position stylistically and will be discussed later.)

"I've Just Seen A Face" is followed by a song even further removed from the rock and roll tradition — "Norwegian Wood": a traditional narrative ballad whose pristine simplicity (including a predominantly acoustic accompaniment and the idiomatically folk-like use of a pedal effect) is interrupted only by the surprising chord that closes the final phrase of the bridge. The third Beatle song written in triple meter, its only links to the rock tradition are an inobtrusive use of percussion and a somewhat problematic use of the *sitar*. While functioning mostly as an "exotic guitar" (Mellers: 63) that doubles the melody, it also provides soft, silvery-toned arpeggios of almost dulcimer-like effect, which contribute to the folk song atmosphere.[4] Furthermore, the lyrics represent one of the clearest examples of the sequential unfolding of a "tale" yet found in the Beatles' output.

Similar in this respect and in their generally folk-like posture are "Girl" and "In My Life," both on Side Two of the American album. The accompaniment of Lennon's composition, "Girl," is again predominantly acoustic and emphasizes the swaying triplet division of the beat more characteristic of folk than rock music at this tempo. The melody is typical of the narrative style in its many repeated notes and primarily conjunct motion, although the Beatles' characteristic use of nonharmonic tones affords the line a sophisticated poignancy not found in most folk songs. The middle section of the song drops its folk-like posture as the triplet division of the beat is replaced by equal eighth notes reinforced by a reiterated background chant. The effect is comparable to the melodramatic recitation style of early rock and roll in its tonic-dominant alternation and results in a definite increase in momentum. The momentum continues as the first section of the song returns with a new guitar counter-melody, which subsequently becomes a solo in an unusually metrical folk-influenced style.

Lennon's "In My Life" evokes the passivity of a restrained folk ballad, eschewing both the blues-derived qualities of the typical pop-rock song and the harmonic suavity and sophistication associated with the slicker commercial ballads. Its generally subdued use of percussion and moderate tempo combine with a then unique section of pseudo-Baroque counterpoint (played by George Martin on piano) and introspective lyrics to evade categorization in the conventional pop genres of the day. Again, the majority of its stylistic indicators suggest the folk ballad, and its credentials in this area are attested to by Judy Collins's subsequent recording.

Like many of its predecessors on *Rubber Soul*, McCartney's "I'm Looking Through You" demonstrates a split personality in its combination and alternation of elements from the pop-rock style and the folk or country-western styles as represented by "I've Just Seen A Face." The acoustic guitar introduction sets the tone with a mixture of folk and country characteristics, which characterize the accompaniment for most of the song. The harmonies are simple and diatonic, lacking any element of surprise. The percussion accompaniment is solid, but strongly suggests the rock and roll idiom only in the final measures of the first section, in which flatted thirds are introduced in the melody and the vocal quality takes on a rock and roll edge. At this point, an electric guitar adds a typical rock riff and the organ (played by Ringo) contributes a few sharply dissonant clusters. The folk-like sound reappears in a brief middle section featuring fragmented country-style guitar interjections. Following this, the more expansive folk-like melody of the first section returns, again interrupted periodically by the starkly contrasting rock and roll gesture described above. Although this stylistic juxtaposition is somewhat less subtle than in previous songs, "I'm Looking Through You" demonstrates many of the same folk-like characteristics as those songs and shares with them a general disregard for the danceable characteristics commonly associated with the pop-rock of the day.

Perhaps the most distinctive example of this disregard for the social dance conventions of rock and roll on *Rubber Soul* is "Michelle." "Michelle" is attributed mainly to Paul McCartney, with

John Lennon given credit for assistance in the middle section. It is, like "Yesterday," an "adult" popular song, an indication of which can be seen in the relatively large number of "cover" versions recorded in the first few months after its release, by performers who appealed primarily to an adult audience.

Mellers states that the model here is "French cabaret song" (ibid.) and, although he gives no concrete examples of that influence, the relationship of the first two chords (I major–iv minor) as well as the augmented sixth chords and harmonic minor scale (the Beatles having previously preferred the aeolian mode or natural minor) are examples of gestures from the decidedly adult tradition of the French chanson. The occasional use of French phrases incorporated effortlessly into the lyrics naturally reinforces this impression. These characteristics are, by themselves, too vague to define the song's character to any great extent, however. "Michelle" is more readily defined as "adult" popular music by its tempo, general mood of restraint, and consistency in the exploitation of adult popular ballad characteristics. Recorded at too rapid a tempo for the traditional rock ballad (an undanceable tempo in that style), it lacks the energy and aggression of the faster rock and roll types. Even the earlier hybrid songs such as "I'm Happy Just to Dance with You" (released as a single in 1964 and appearing also on both versions of the *A Hard Day's Night* album) contained several direct references to the rock and roll idiom (especially in the role played by guitar and percussion) lacking in "Michelle."

"Popular" melodic-harmonic elements have, of course, always played an important role in the Beatles' pop-rock style, but here these elements are presented in their original context, undiluted by elements from the blues-derived rock and roll tradition. Chromatic sequences as in "Michelle" take on widely divergent meanings when played by the quietly mellow electric guitar and soft, pattering percussion, or by the energetic, biting guitar and percussion combination found in so many other Beatle songs. By eliminating almost all aspects of rock instrumentation and energy, and by focusing the commercial, popular elements of their musical vocabulary, the Beatles succeeded in producing a successful "adult" song — one which may also have achieved popularity among the young but whose relationship to the social dance tradition of their generation is minimal.

While the songs discussed up to this point all, for varying reasons, fall outside the social dance tradition (unlike virtually all previous Beatle compositions), some songs on *Rubber Soul* modify typical rock and roll dance styles rather than depart from them. In this category is Lennon's "It's Only Love," one of the two songs to appear first on the British *Help!* album. "It's Only Love" mixes the rock ballad style and the up-tempo or moderate tempo rock and roll style similar in many respects to that found in some earlier Beatle songs, but exhibits a greater modification of those traditional styles in its approach to momentum, complexity, and musical detail.

The outstanding manifestation of this complexity and detail is the multiplicity of sounds and tone colors in the instrumental accompaniment. Six different guitar effects appear, ranging from a vigorous acoustic strum to a tremolo on the electric lead guitar. The various individual and combined effects are made possible by the most extensive multiple tracking to be found on any early Beatle album; this degree of detail in instrumentation in itself indicates an artistic intent the self-consciousness of which is precedented by few of the Beatles' earlier compositions ("Yesterday" being a possible exception).

Also indicating a stress on values not formerly associated with the social dance tradition of rock and roll is the ambiguity of momentum and continuity created by conflict between the square, regular rhythm of the unusually legato lyrical melody of the first section and its actively syncopated instrumental accompaniment. This contrast — far greater than in most of the earlier hybrids — results in a virtual duality of momentum between the two levels. This duality of momentum is reinforced by the duality of melodic-harmonic style, which combines elements of both the Beatles' commercial popular vocabulary and their rock ballad style (cf. "Yesterday"). "It's Only Love" thus represents a further expansion of the Beatles' rock idiom — perhaps the result of their increasing desire to create music as free as possible from the limiting context of mid-sixties' rock and roll.

However significant a break with the rock and roll tradition may be represented by several of the songs on *Rubber Soul*, the album does not demonstrate a complete break with the past, as clearly shown by the three following songs. Each of these songs shows, albeit in varying degrees of prominence, qualities characteristic of the rock and roll tradition of the mid-sixties.

McCartney's "You Won't See Me" features a pop-rock atmosphere generated mostly by the instrumental accompaniment. Virtually all of its instrumental and vocal activities appear to be securely in the mainstream rock and roll tradition, but the song also contains some subtle distortions of that tradition. The "ooh-la-la-la" vocal accompaniment must be heard as parody, given its history of use in the fifties. Furthermore, the apparent reason for the vocal fill — the significant pauses within the melodic phrases — is in itself somewhat uncharacteristic of rock style. While the frenzied vocal activities in the recordings of Little Richard (and in the Beatles' "I'm Down," among others) may not have represented the general prototype for the Beatles' songs, it is clear that a certain amount of vocal energy had traditionally been a key factor in establishing the momentum associated with the successful up-tempo rock and roll songs in the dance tradition of the sixties. Precisely this vocal energy is missing in the Beatles' recording of "You Won't See Me."

Based partially on syncopated melodic-rhythmic material similar to that in "You Won't See Me," McCartney's "Wait" goes further in exploring the conflict between syncopation and silence in such a way as to create a constant fluctuation in momentum. While the chorus and middle section of the song display a traditional pop-rock continuity, the primary section is characterized by rhythmic stops and starts, which disrupt the metric regularity associated with that style.

While the two preceding songs demonstrate relatively subtle aberrations within the pop-rock idiom, the final three songs to be discussed may be considered virtual prototypes of the Beatles' more traditional work. George Harrison's "Think for Yourself" employs tambourine, maracas, and drum set along with a "fuzz" bass, regular bass guitar, eighth note block chords on organ or electric piano, and electric lead guitar to generate a full and energetic up-tempo pop-rock accompaniment. This is paired with a vocal melody well suited to the accompaniment, even though it is also quite typical of Harrison's later work in its drooping, often three-part vocal line replete with nonharmonic tones. The song is set in a verse-chorus pattern in which the latter exhibits an increase in momentum due to the heavier activity in fuzz bass and percussion, and a melody line closely related to the instrumental riff found in the Beatles' earlier recording of "Money" (*The Beatles' Second Album*, 1964) in its pedal-like repetition against changing chords.

Like Harrison's composition, Lennon and McCartney's "The Word" stands firmly in the rock and roll tradition while exhibiting a few eccentricities. In instrumental sound, "The Word" appears at first to be patterned after the typical blues-rock style of the white blues bands of the mid-sixties (cf. The Paul Butterfield Blues Band's recording of "Get Out My Life Woman" on *East-West*). The middle section introduces some new elements, however. The three-note lead guitar melody is closely related to the middle section vocal melody in "Think for Yourself" and, like it, acts as a stable pedal element under which the harmony changes. Also pedal-like in effect are the harmonium open fifths (played by George Martin), which appear in an instrumental bridge section before and after the vocal coda. Melodically, the song is more conventional, with the first section emphasizing the juxtaposition of major and minor tonic chords, which characterizes many blues and blues-rock songs.

"Run for Your Life" is a Lennon composition of which little

need be said. Based on the durable rock cliche of I-vi alternation, the song contains only two different phrases — a four-measure phrase associated with the verse and a two-measure phrase associated with the chorus. The country-western-inspired lead guitar solo is typical of many such Beatle pop-rock tunes, and only a consistent use of unusual nonharmonic tones lends a hint of distinction to the song.

The basically traditional nature of the last three songs notwithstanding, the American version of *Rubber Soul* clearly represents a new departure in the Beatles' music insofar as it demands a redefinition of most of its material in a context unrelated to the traditional social dance function previously considered germane to rock and roll. Whereas earlier Beatle experimentation had generally been concerned with innovations of harmony, melody, and — to a lesser degree — instrumentation, in *Rubber Soul* The Beatles moved to deny the very social and functional origins of rock and roll and demanded that their music be experienced exclusively through the aural process. This is not to suggest that the Beatles' music on *Rubber Soul* cannot be or has not been danced to, but rather to assert that the music is no longer primarily concerned with expediting the dance.

Furthermore, most of the songs contained on the album are unified in their demonstration of a new approach to rock and roll — an approach that focuses on musical detail rather than on the massive, ear-catching sound gestures of the earlier pop-rock songs. This disregard for the traditional requirements of simplicity, massive effects, and dance potential was manifest in some earlier Beatle compositions, but no previous album was so consistent in its denial of commercial conventions. This disregard may, paradoxically, have been made feasible only by the absolute guarantee of commercial success for any Beatle venture in 1965, and the relatively generous amount of studio recording time justified thereby.

A second specifically musical attribute shared by several songs on *Rubber Soul* involves those compositions that may be classified as country, folk, or a combination of the two in terms of the influences they display. Both country and folk elements were, of course, contained in earlier Beatle songs, but only as modifiers of the pop-rock tradition, not as a main component or main stylistic feature.

The Beatles' intention was not, in any case, to produce folk or country music, but rather to consolidate it with pop-rock to produce a hybrid form rather than merely a folk or country-flavored rock and roll song as in their earlier years. Neither the disregard for the conventions of commercial rock and roll nor the pre-occupation with musical detail necessarily presupposes a turn toward these styles; rather, the country and folk styles are used simply as a source for melodic-harmonic material and sound ideas that had not been drained of their potential for originality by over-exposure on the popular market. Country and folk music styles had been familiar to the Beatles for many years, and it is understandable that their first attempt to break from the stiff requirements of the commercial rock and roll market should draw heavily on them in many cases.

Still, the Beatles' experimentation with folk and country music had little effect on the well-established folk-rock style of the sixties, which was still primarily concerned with dance suitability. The folk-rock groups, as exemplified by the American group, the Byrds, opted for a more substantial and aggressive rock accompaniment featuring a solid, eminently danceable beat. Compared to the music of the Byrds and their many imitators, the Beatles' understated style on *Rubber Soul* was, with its subtle instrumental backings and demure stylistic borrowings from folk and country music, almost tantamount to a return to "purity."

Furthermore, the Beatles did not seem particularly anxious to further pursue the folk and country-influenced genre they had created. In *Rubber Soul* they managed to achieve great popular success while violating many tenets of the "Top Forty" tradition. (None of the songs of *Rubber Soul* were released as singles, although several received air-play on AM radio, notably "Michelle.") They showed an unprecedented lack of concern for the dance-oriented restrictions of the period and made of their music something that seemed fit more for listening than for dancing. Having accomplished this, the Beatles soon proved themselves equal to other conquests. And yet, I doubt that any of these future conquests truly surpasses the subtle triumph of *Rubber Soul.*

NOTES

1.   The term "ballad" is used here to denote those songs characterized by sustained, lyrical melodies at relatively slow tempi, generally with texts of a romantic-sentimental type.

2.   All compositional attributions cited here are taken from Meller's useful book.

3.   "Country-western" is meant here to refer to the repertoire that, in the sixties, would have been listed on the commercial record charts under that category. This would include music by performers such as Buck Owens, Porter Wagoner, and others, and generally features a flat, nasal vocal tone, often with vocal harmony in thirds, and a relatively simple and repetitive melodic and harmonic structure, usually without the accented rhythmic patterns and syncopation that characterize rock and roll.

4.   "Folk" here refers to songs thus characterized by the popular music industry in the sixties. Recorded by performers such as Bob Dylan and Peter, Paul, and Mary, they usually include a predominantly acoustic guitar accompaniment, as well as some of the melodic and strophic elements associated with traditional American-English folk songs and ballads. More "popular" elements may also be present, especially in the instrumental accompaniment.

REFERENCE CITED

Mellers, Wilfrid
    1973   *Twilight of the Gods: The Music of the Beatles.* N.Y.: Viking.

DISCOGRAPHY

(Listed Chronologically)

The Beatles' Second Album. Capitol ST 2309. Recording: London, 1963 and 1964; release: April, 1964; producer: George Martin.

A Hard Day's Night. United Artists UAS 3366A (American version), Parlophone PSC 3058 (British version). Recording: London, 1964; release: June, 1964 (American), August, 1964 (British); producer: George Martin.

"I'm Down." (Single) Capitol 5476 (American), Parlophone PCS 3071 (British). Recording: London, 1964; release: July, 1965; producer: George Martin.

Help! Capitol SMAS 2386 (American), Parlophone PCS 3071 (British). Recording: London, 1965; release: August, 1965; producer: George Martin.

Rubber Soul. Capitol ST 2442 (American), Parlophone PCS 3075 (British). Recording: London, 1965; release: December, 1965; producer: George Martin.

East-West (The Paul Butterfield Blues Band). Elektra 315. Release: 1966.

Introduction to
SUSTAINED PERFORMANCES:
"SGT. PEPPER'S LONELY HEARTS CLUB BAND"

The effect of **Sergeant Pepper's Lonely Hearts Club Band** upon the rock-and-roll album as an art form is immeasurable. It involved the highest production values, the most imaginative cover art and the most cohesive lyrical content of any Beatles album to date. And to insure that the audience would notice the lyrics, which loosely tell the story of a performance by Sergeant Pepper's band, they printed the words, like a libretto, on the back of the album cover. Here, from *Beowulf to Beatles, Approaches to Poetry*, David R. Pichaske examines the lyrics as a long work of poetry, the pop music equivalent of Edgar Lee Masters' *Spoon River Anthology* or A.E. Housman's *A Shropshire Lad.*

SUSTAINED PERFORMANCES:
"SGT. PEPPER'S LONELY HEARTS CLUB BAND"

by David R. Pichaske

The more one listens to *Sergeant Pepper*, the more carefully one analyzes the imagery and the almost infinite variety of rhythm and rhyme, the more one hears other albums by other rock groups, the more stunning this album becomes. Musically and verbally it was impressive when it first appeared; in retrospect it is even more impressive. There can be little doubt that it will be listened to and studied for many years to come, because of both the quality of its music and the variety of its poetry.

The long-playing record imposes itself as a form upon The Beatles' work, of course, and they must work within its context: the performance may not extend much beyond an hour, but at least forty minutes of time must be filled. The public expects a series of single cuts on each side; the first and last cuts will have emphasis because of their positions. There will be a break at the end of the first side, which may necessitate some form of recapitulation at the beginning of the second. Within these predetermined confines, however, The Beatles are free to develop a narrative (as The Who did with *Tommy*) or thematically related lyrics that work off each other. They compromise: the two "Sergeant Pepper" songs frame a series of distinct studies of great musical and poetry variety, putting the whole album in the context of a stage performance (the illusion is furthered by "A Little Help From My Friends"). The last cut on the second side is parenthetical, outside the performance context, a new perspective on all that has gone before.

The place to begin a consideration of the album is with the individual lyrics, some of which have already been the subject of considerable discussion. Only after one has grasped the songs individually can one begin drawing patterns of meaning from the whole album. "Lucy In the Sky" is widely interpreted as an acid trip and an acrostic for LSD. Certainly both the tonal distortions of the music and the rich sensual imagery of the poem suggest the popular conception of such a trip. Moreover, the boat, the taxi, and the train all suggest "trip" in the literal sense, and the distortions in sense perception evidenced by the tall flowers past which one drifts, the intense awareness of color and taste in tangerine trees and marmalade skies, and the hallucinations hinted at by "rocking horse people" and Lucy's kaleidoscope eyes would seemingly settle the issue. But in an interview in the *Washington Post*, Paul McCartney claimed that the song derived from a picture drawn by John Lennon's little boy, Julian. Although he could not deny the appropriateness of the LSD interpretation, he claimed that in writing the poem they had never thought about that at all. It may, of course, be that the interview rather than the song was a put-on, but one is never sure. "Lucy In the Sky" is a powerful poem even if it is not an acid song: the title image suggests an awareness that the rest of the song develops, an awareness of the most common of things in the most uncommon of contexts, imbueing Lucy with mystical attraction. Perhaps the song is really about the awareness of the extraordinary within the ordinary — but then that is precisely what LSD is reported (perhaps erroneously) to open one's eyes to.

"For the Benefit of Mr. Kite" presents another problem. McCartney claimed it came straight off a wall poster; others remind us that kiff (pot) and hashish — Mssrs. K. and H. whose performance will be second to none — and horse are all slang terms for drugs, and argue for a drug interpretation. After all, H. turns somesets without ever leaving the ground, and K. flies through a ring. Perhaps the circus imagery is but an adjunct to describing a trip. Or perhaps the drug images and the circus images supplement each other, both functioning metaphorically to suggest a further, deeper theme: the loss of one's self (with related anxieties, self-analyses, and doubts) in the magic of a grand performance. Drugs take one away from reality for a moment just as the carnival atmosphere of a circus takes one away; one loses hold of reality in the noise and color and magic of the moment. And certainly Mister Kite's performance is a splendid, colorful, swirling, enchanting thing metrically as well as imagistically.

"A Day in the Life" is, with the possible exception of "Lucy in the Sky," the most haunting and the most ambiguous song on the album. Madison Avenue has managed to make the phrase "turn on" virtually meaningless by applying it to everything from shades of cosmetics to chocolate malts, but the expression always did have a certain ambiguity to it. First, of course, it means drugs, and the man is having a smoke and the Beatles have admitted in various interviews to using various drugs and the B.B.C. was convinced enough of the line's meaning to ban the song from the network. But the other images in the song suggest that we are being asked to turn on to an awareness of the bankruptcy of life as we usually live it in the twentieth century, and to an awareness of what life might be. The man blew his mind out just when he finally made the grade, the war was won but nobody really cared. Life goes on, a collage of nearly missed buses and holes to be carefully counted. If "Lucy in the Sky" was a trip that turned us on to the magic of what is conventional, all that magic has disappeared in "A Day in the Life." The trip is over, and it was a bummer.

The comparison between these two songs brings us to a more important question: what kind of a statement does the album as a whole make? Everyone, including for a change McCartney himself, agrees that yes, it does have a unity, and it is obvious that the unity is intentional: "Sergeant Pepper's Lonely Hearts Club Band" introduces Billy Shears and "With A Little Help"; the record moves without a break from the end of "Sergeant Pepper's (Reprise)" to "A Day in the Life"; the drug motif repeats itself again and again in the "high" of "A Little Help," the weeds of "When I'm Sixty-Four," the tea of "Lovely Rita." Technically, the crescendo at the end of "A Day in the Life" is an analog of the barnyard cacophony at the end of "Good Morning," just as the emptiness of the imagery reflects the same banality implicit in the other. "Within You Without You" proclaims overtly what the previous lyrics suggested indirectly; it is a kind of summary of side one of the album before we begin side two. "When I'm Sixty-Four" balances "She's Leaving Home." And so on. But what kind of a statement does this unity make?

The context of the whole album is provided by the opening two songs: this is a performance by Sergeant Pepper (Ringo Star,* alias Billy Shears — he wears the sergeant's stripes on his uniform) and his lonely hearts club band. Two things are important: the band is lonely, and it is performing. Perhaps the two are interrelated: performers are generally lonely people, lonely people perform when they pretend not to be lonely and in an attempt to escape their loneliness. What is especially significant, however, is that Sergeant Pepper and his band are aware of the fact that they are performing, that they are acting out an illusion — others are not as aware, but then again they are probably not as lonely. Some are off into a drug thing; others tell themselves that things are, after all, getting better all the time, or rationalize their disillusionment by excusing themselves. Some withdraw into self-isolation and others drown any misgivings they might have in the noise and excitement of a circus performance. "What we were talking about," says George Harrison bluntly in "Within You Without You," "is what is hypocritical and what is honest, and who hides behind what walls of illusion." But if the lyrics of this song outline inadequate responses people make when they are vaguely aware that something is wrong with their lives, the next three songs present us with a gallery of incredibly shallow individuals.

----

*Editor's note: The proper spelling is "Starr."

The first proposes the most mundane of marriages to a mail-order bride; the second falls in love with a meter maid he happens to see writing up tickets; the third drives in self-impressed fashion aimlessly around town looking for pick-ups. What makes the whole despicable crowd especially disgusting (and The Beatles' comment especially morose) is the irrepressible high spirits of the music, which ironically mocks the words themselves and piles irony on top of irony. And then the band, Sergeant Pepper's Band, Sergeant Pepper's Lonely Hearts Club Band, breaks in with its initial statement, now made depressingly meaningful: "Sergeant Pepper's lonely." The "l" is lower case; the phrase ends with a period. The band is making a statement: "Sergeant Pepper is lonely," and that's what we've been talking about for the duration of this performance. By now we as listeners have begun to feel a trifle lonely too, and "A Day In the Life," with the alienated, impassive attitude of the observers and its resounding chord dying-out-to-nothing at the end is almost too much. But it is too much not simply because of the song itself, but because the entire weight of the whole album comes crashing down on that final chord. And the whole weight of *Sergeant Pepper* is a lot of weight.

Introduction to
ROCK AND FINE ART

The Beatles, the White Album. Fans love it. Fans hate it. Carl Belz appreciates it as a self-conscious statement of the musical styles that influenced the Beatles. His book, *The Story of Rock* (Oxford University Press, 1969), traces the history of rock-and-roll and concludes with the following review of **The Beatles** as it reflects its musical past and stands outside the evolution of rock music.

Here Belz explains how he came to write "Rock and Fine Art" in the fall of 1968: "The manuscript had been accepted by Oxford, but I was in the process of doing a lot of rewriting, getting it ready for publication. Quite separately, and as a part of my teaching interests, I was reading a lot about Manet and modernist painting (my training is in art history). Then one day one of my students brought in the White Album hot off the press (I seem to recall that a certain amount of status was in those days associated with getting a new album before anyone else . . .) and . . . my seminar . . . sat down and listened to the whole thing from start to finish. Well, it all came together, and I mean ALL . . . folk art, fine art, the whole thing . . . ."

ROCK AND FINE ART

by Carl Belz

Since its release, the Beatles' 1968 album has provoked extensive controversy. It has been called a "put-down" and a "put-on" and it has been said to represent the Beatles' way of "dropping out" of the rock picture. These judgments are related to a superficially disturbing aspect of the album itself: the fact that it contains references to the overall history of rock music. That is, many of its songs are openly derived from earlier rock, from the Beach Boys, Chuck Berry, Bob Dylan, and even the Beatles' own records; and from trends such as Country and Western, Rhythm and Blues, popular folk, folk-rock, acid rock, electronic rock, psychedelic rock and others that have appeared during the 1960's. But the references are used loosely; few songs on the ablum are based exclusively on one past rock style. "Back In The U.S.S.R." contains musical allusions to both Chuck Berry and the Beach Boys; "Birthday" is lyrically reminiscent of a long tradition of songs dealing with the same subject, while its instrumentation frantically obscures the lyrics in the manner of such classics as the Kingsmen's "Louie, Louie"; "Rocky Raccoon" refers at once to Bob Dylan's early style and to the tradition of country music narratives generally. Other links to the past are numerous: "Me And My Monkey" and "Helter Skelter" both have a heavy, acid-rock orientation; "Yer Blues" and "Why Don't We Do It In The Road" are clear examples of the Negro blues tradition; "Martha My Dear" and "Honey Pie" express the camp sensibility which has brought about a revival of the 1930's; and "I Will," "Blackbird" and "Julia" are like the tender ballads of the early Beatles, for instance "If I Fell" and "Do You Want To Know A Secret."

To many listeners, these references to the past are disturbing because they envision the Beatles as rock music's *avant garde*, as the signal for each new direction; for these listeners, the Beatles have suddenly "dropped out" of the rock evolution. Moreover, the Beatles have invariably been viewed as the most sophisticated of rock groups.

Their return to the music of earlier periods therefore seems inconsistent with their previous development away from it. Because of this seeming inconsistency, listeners have concluded that the Beatles must either be "putting down" earlier rock or "putting on" their own audience, joking with them about the musical fads of the past.

Actually, the Beatles are not entirely alone in their enterprise. During 1968, there were several events which indicated a comparable direction in the overall rock movement. Earlier, I mentioned the album, *John Wesley Harding* by Bob Dylan,* and I pointed out that the record shows a return to Dylan's earlier lyric and instrumental style. As in *The Beatles*, such a return implies a critical disengagement from the concept of rock "progress," a concept which has been applied to Dylan almost as frequently as it has to the Beatles. Still, the self-awareness of Dylan's music is not as blatant as that of *The Beatles*, nor does it compel recognition with the same authority. It is not insisted upon.

The 1968 album, *Cruising With Ruben And The Jets*, by Frank Zappa and the Mothers of Invention, also involves a conscious return to earlier rock music, particularly to the ballad style of the 1950's and the early 1960's, to Little Caesar and the Romans, for instance, the Flamingos, Don Julian and the Meadowlarks and the Jaguars. And the songs on the album were all written by Zappa and his group. They are not merely revival versions of Oldies But Goodies, although in style they could easily be mistaken for their historical counterparts whereas the Beatles' 1968 songs could not. A fascinating aspect of *Cruising With Ruben And The Jets* concerns the album notes. They include "The Story of Ruben and the Jets," an amusing, tongue-in-cheek description of a (fictitious?) rock group of the 1950's; but they also contain a direct statement of intention on the part of the Mothers of Invention, namely that the record was created out of respect for the style of music it emulates. Against the experience of the album itself, however, this statement seems odd. The music does not elicit respect for rock history in the way that the written statement insists it should, or in the way that *The Beatles* elicits respect for its own sources. It appears to have a mixed response toward the past, finding quality in it on the one hand, but feeling embarrassment about it on the other. And the album notes which claim to "really like" old rock ballads also call them "greasy love songs" characterized by "cretin simplicity." The ambivalence of this statement parallels the ambivalence of Frank Zappa's music. By comparison, the Beatles' songs are in no way ambivalent in their treatment of rock history.

I want to argue that the Beatles' return to the past is neither a

----

*Editor's note: By "earlier," Belz means earlier in the book *The Story of Rock*.

"put-down" nor a "put-on," but an expression of consciousness which is unprecedented in the history of rock and which defines the 1968 album as fine art. Specifically, it is a consciousness of the fact that the record is, after all, a record. That is, the album is nonmetaphoric: Its primary purpose is not to talk about the world, create pictures of it, or refer to specific experiences within it. The primary purpose of *The Beatles* is to present a conscious experience of music as music.

The record's consciousness of itself is shown in many ways. In the first place, the variety of its songs presents a singular, unified subject: rock music as it has existed and changed during a decade and a half. More precisely, the subject of the record is rock history as experienced by the Beatles. What is their attitude to rock on this record? The evidence suggests that the Beatles have a profound respect for the music which provides their subject matter. The Beatles do not use album notes to "explain" their intentions. The question about their attitude toward rock can only be answered by what a listener feels is the aesthetic quality of the songs in the album. Each song, it seems to me, implies respect for its subject because it is a fine interpretation of that subject — that is, of each example in the spectrum of rock sub-styles. Songs derived from the Beach Boys have an elegant harmony; the Chuck Berry inspirations are rocking, explosive and humorous; the Rhythm and Blues examples have a direct and heavy beat; and the Beatle-style ballads are tender and restrained. The songs isolate and emphasize the best musical aspects of their subjects. They do not imply that their musical subject matter is inane, insignificant, or in any way embarrassing. Only the listener who personally feels embarrassment about the songs he formerly liked can interpret the Beatles' album as sharing that response. But such an interpretation results from arbitrarily reading into the album instead of accepting musical evidence from it.

In this album, the Beatles are going back over musical territory which they have already covered, which they already know, and which they have left. The consiousness with which they look back is significant for the history of rock because it has been transformed into artistic content. In part, the transformation is achieved by the overtness with which the past is used. That is, it is most immediate and most real at those moments when the listener clearly recognizes that the record does in fact involve a return to the past. Listeners who are not aware of either rock history or the Beatles' own past, are not likely to grasp this. In other words, the sophistication manifested by so many aspects of sixties rock becomes, in the case of the Beatles' 1968 album, a literal prerequisite for understanding the record's full content and historical significance — although not necessarily for feeling some of its aesthetic impact; it is a great record, even for listeners who do not know what it means in terms of rock history. In comparison to *The Beatles*, an awareness of Chuck Berry, the Beach Boys, and other rock artists was never the *content* of the Beatles' early songs. Those artists were simply influences on them. In the 1968 album, they are recognized *as* influences, and this recognition or consciousness openly pervades the entire record and becomes its content. Moreover, because *The Beatles* is aware of itself, it cannot be regarded as a revival of the past or an imitation of it. As a musical statement, the album clearly belongs to the Beatles; its overall style is consistent with the group's previous development, although it extends that development into a new area.

Consistency between the Beatles' 1968 album and their earlier records is evident in several ways. Like *Rubber Soul, Revolver* and particularly *Sgt. Pepper, The Beatles* has an extraordinary range and extraordinary inventiveness. Lyrically, the songs shift from the straightforward "Julia," "I Will" or "Dear Prudence," to the elusive and quasi-surrealistic "Glass Onion" and "Happiness Is A Warm Gun"; the lyrics also range from simple narrative in "Rocky Raccoon" to virtual anti-narrative in "Why Don't We Do It In The Road," which consists merely of three lines, two of which are identical; in addition, they include numerous expressions of humor as in "Back In The U.S.S.R.," "Ob-La-Di, Ob-La-Da," and "The Continuing Story of Bungalow Bill"; and, in George Harrison's "Piggies," social commentary. The range of writing in *The Beatles* is unprecedented in either past or present rock history. Moreover, such virtuoso writing underscores the album's consciousness: It summarizes the richness and variety of rock lyrics as they have existed in the idiom up to, and including, the present.

The same virtuosity is apparent in the music of *The Beatles*. As I said, it covers the history of rock sub-styles and influences. Yet, each of these is clearly personalized by the English group as they at once acknowledge the past and place upon it their unique stylistic stamp. Whether rock ("Back In The U.S.S.R.") or blues ("Yer Blues"), country ("Rocky Raccoon") or ballad ("I Will"), each song combines ease with restraint, resulting in the cool refinement which has become characteristic of the Beatles' music during the past five years. Moreover, there are no "repeats" in the album. Each of the softer ballads makes a distinct impact, and the same is true of the rock numbers, the psychedelic numbers, and the thirties reminiscences. No other group has been able to move so authoritatively through such a varied texture of rock expressions.

Still, the lyric and musical virtuosity of *The Beatles* is not simply an end in itself. The album is not a narcissistic "demonstration piece" which intends to show the rock world that the Beatles are more accomplished than any other group. Certainly, it can be accepted this way, but to do so would undermine the impact of the album as an aesthetic experience in itself, and it would imply that the Beatles had turned their backs on the meaning of creativity expressed by their earlier work — as if their purpose was now to minimize other groups when it had never been their purpose before. It seems to me that neither effect is substantiated by the album itself. Rather, I think that the virtuosity in *The Beatles* serves the purpose of making a statement about rock music: It validates the extraordinary range and power of rock expressions. Such a statement could not be made unless the Beatles had the musical ability to produce songs which were as varied and good as their subjects. So the album does mark a new phase in the Beatles' enterprise. In their records before 1968, they were learning what rock consisted of and they were learning to make their own brand of rock music. But *The Beatles* involves a breakthrough: a conscious looking back at their own musical experiences.

The Beatles' album *can* be regarded as a "drop out," but not in the sense that most listeners suppose. They have questioned the idea of progress in rock music. During the late sixties, rock has been looked upon as becoming more advanced, more sophisticated, more electronic, and more like fine art than it was in the past. The Beatles' record asks, "Is it necessarily becoming *better*?" They have questioned whether progress and artistic quality are the same. The Beatles have experienced an undeniable artistic quality in earlier rock *in spite* of the fact that the previous music was *not* advanced, sophisticated, electronic or like fine art. But *The Beatles* has this meaning only to the extent that it possesses high quality itself. In other words, the album relies on quality alone to substantiate its vision.

The equation of progress and quality is characteristic of the folk mentality. In many cases, progress is tangible and immediate; it can be pinpointed, isolated and demonstrated. Unconscious folk artists and audiences do not realize how these features may imply quality in technology, say, without implying quality in art. A marked tendency in the sixties is to say that rock has become art because it is complex, because it is technically accomplished, or because it contains references to fine art — that is, to Stockhausen, Cage, Mozart, Bach and other composers who are acknowledged to represent fine art. In addition, it is suggested that freedom of interpretation and far ranging instrumental improvisation constitute fine art. Examples of these tendencies are Cream, Vanilla Fudge, and the Jimi Hendrix Experience. But these are folk claims: They equate sophistication with quality, just as they equate progress with quality.

The Beatles' consciousness of itself as music is not just suggested, it is compelled. In the song "Ob-La-Di, Ob-La-Da," for instance, the lyrics concern a married couple named Desmond and Molly, but, in describing the lives of Desmond and Molly, they arbitrarily interchange the names so that neither person can be established as the husband or wife. The effect is amusing and disturbing, but only if one regards the song as being directly *about* people in the world. It is nonmetaphoric: it is primarily a good *song*. "Revolution 1" sings about revolution and changing the world. The lyrics are identical to the lyrics of "Revolution," a single released by the Beatles before their 1968 album. The difference between the two versions lies in the way they are sung: "Revolution" is a fast, rocking record, but "Revolution 1" is performed slowly, as though the first song had been decelerated to half-speed. And the album also contains "Revolution 9," which is almost entirely an electronic, tape-music composition. So, are they *about* revolution? I want to argue that, as much as Claude Monet's paintings of haystacks or Frank Stella's stripe paintings are about painting, "Revolution 1," "Revolution," and "Revolution 9" are about music. They constitute a series for which the subject of revolution is a common denominator, a constant, or a "control," so to speak, which merely functions as a point of reference for the primary concern, the music.

There are other ways in which *The Beatles* stresses the experience of itself as music. The lyrics for all the songs are printed on a separate sheet that is included with the album. The Beatles first did this with *Sgt. Pepper*, where the lyrics are printed on the album itself. In both cases, the gesture obviates the task of "figuring out" what the lyrics actually are — the task that rock listeners were traditionally confronted with prior to the Beatles. Admittedly, it can be argued that printing the lyrics in this fashion actually adds to their importance as "poetry" which exists independently of music. Certainly, this is the case with Bob Dylan's albums, several of which contain "poems" which are distinct from the ones on the recording, but whose similarity to them lends the songs a "poetic" significance. With the Beatles, however, knowing the lyrics seems to facilitate listening to the music; it enables the music to exist by itself, unencumbered by efforts to grasp the words and intellectualize their "meaning." Those activities can take place when the record is not being played.

In addition to "Ob-La-Di, Ob-La-Da," "Revolution 1," and "Revolution 9," several other songs serve to emphasize the self-contained musical experience of *The Beatles*. For instance, "Back In The U.S.S.R." presents a subject that, for most listeners, is nonsensical, although certainly humorous, if it is related to extra-musical realities. "Glass Onion" also restricts the listener from making direct associations between musical experience and nonmusical experience. Its lyrics openly refer to other Beatles songs — "Strawberry Fields,"

"I Am The Walrus" and "Lady Madonna" — but they suggest that the effort to interpret those songs via the context of ordinary, day-to-day experiences is absurd, like "fixing a hole in the ocean." For the Beatles, in other words, music elicits its own kind of experience, one that is valid by itself and requires no justification through references to the nonmusical world. Thus, at a moment when rock writers are increasingly anxious to make meaningful and intelligent statements about the world, the Beatles have chosen to investigate their own musical experiences. Such a decision is daring, but it is consistent with the unique position the Beatles have occupied ever since they entered the rock picture.

The Beatles' transformation of consciousness into content has a clear parallel in the history of fine art, particularly in the history of modernist painting. In painting, a comparable breakthrough was achieved by Edouard Manet. Manet made the distancing experience of consciousness the content of his work; he blatantly used the art of the past as his subject matter rather than allowing it merely to influence him; he acknowledged the quality of earlier art, and he recognized that his personal contribution as a painter could only be substantiated if it was good; finally, he was accused of "putting down" the history of his medium and of "putting on" the audience of French art.* Modernist painting has directly and indirectly explored the implications of Manet's art for more than a century. This fact should lend caution to predictions that rock music will suddenly follow the Beatles' direction.

I have tried to emphasize the Beatles' 1968 album in terms of its consciousness and, correspondingly, its fine art identity. In doing so, I am aware of alternative interpretations of the record's meaning, particularly those interpretations which might stress the album's links with its folk past. Admittedly, not all of the songs insist upon nonmetaphoric listening with the same authority. Moreover, the album's internal richness and complexity thwart attempts to straightjacket all of its parts into a single, rigid viewpoint. From the point of view of this book, however, the album's art-consciousness constitutes its major historical achievement. And that achievement matters for one all-important reason: It is couched in supremely good music.

---

*For a discussion of Manet, see the special issue of *Artforum* (March 1969), by Michael Fried. — C.B.

FURTHER READING
PART II

Probably the definitive work on Beatles albums, *The Beatles, An Illustrated Record* (Harmony Books, 1975, revised 1978 and 1981), by Roy Carr and Tony Tyler, reviews every disk officially released from 1962 on. Although the 1981 edition tends to hurry through the more pale solo efforts, the book is an excellent record-by-record history of the Beatles.

For those who ever wondered which Beatle played the maracas on *Hello Goodbye*, the complete discography *All Together Now* (Pierian Press, 1975; Ballantine Books, 1976), by Harry Castleman and Walter J. Podrazik, is so complete that it contains a section giving such information. The authors conceded, however, that it was not complete enough and produced the supplement *The Beatles Again!?* (Pierian Press, 1977), and third sequel, *The End of the Beatles* (Pierian Press, 1984) to finish the job! Who did play maracas on *Hello Goodbye*? The answer, from page 160 of *All Together Now*: Ringo.

Producer George Martin discusses the creation of Beatles records in his autobiography *All You Need Is Ears* (St. Martin's, 1979), written with Jeremy Hornsby. The "fifth Beatle" of the Abbey Road studio number two, Martin explains how he and the group achieved effects on songs like *Tomorrow Never Knows, Strawberry Fields Forever* and *A Day in the Life*. As a supplement, see *Out of His Head: The Sound of Phil Spector* (Outerbridge and Lazard, 1972), by Richard Williams. Chapter Nine tells how the legendary producer of the Ronettes and the Crystals salvaged the "Let It Be" tapes and came to produce albums for John Lennon and George Harrison.

Part III
Varied Critical Viewpoints

Introduction to
THE BALLAD STYLE IN
THE EARLY MUSIC OF THE BEATLES

Terence J. O'Grady contributes again with "The Ballad Style in the Early Music of the Beatles." Here he examines the use of ballads in the Beatles' early recording career (1962–1965) and theorizes why they chose to record ballads by established composers (*Till There Was You, A Taste of Honey*) when Lennon and McCartney were already creating beautiful, mature works for singer Cilla Black (*It's for You, Love of the Loved*) and others.

THE BALLAD STYLE IN
THE EARLY MUSIC OF THE BEATLES

by Terence J. O'Grady

The role of popular music in the college curriculum has always been somewhat vague and ill-defined. When, in the late 1960s, college courses in popular music were added to the traditional offerings in western art music, ethnomusicology, and jazz, the action seemed to be taken more as a response to the then frequent demand for relevance than for any specific pedagogical reasons, or because of any well-developed view that the study of popular music filled some important gap or in some way complemented the more traditional areas of musical endeavor. The cries for relevance, as useful and productive as they have been in some areas, seem to have diminished somewhat in recent years. Perhaps it is now appropriate to examine more carefully the *musical* relevance of popular music to the college curriculum.

The study of popular music is, perhaps before anything else, an ethnomusicological one. The "commercial" concerns of popular music do not diminish its potential as a social indicators; on the contrary, it is just these concerns, coupled with the "trendiness" of the genre and its suitability for dissemination in a mass culture, that make it such a valuable barometer of society. Popular music clearly has a place in ethnomusicological studies, right alongside the broadside ballads and the music of the street-singing Bauls of Bengal.

And yet, any approach to popular music which investigates only its social milieu would be failing to take into account its instructive value in purely musical terms. It is specifically the *music* of popular music which is too often neglected, whether the focus is on the popular music of another era, or on contemporary popular music. All too frequently, popular music criticism deals at length with the sociological implications of the lyrics, hair length, sadistic role-playing in performance, etc., and the musical aspects are glossed over. This is not to suggest that a musical analysis of popular music is likely to shed much light on art music for those not kindly disposed to it. The differences in context between popular music and art music are as great, or possibly greater, than between the art musics of

79

non-western cultures. We do not study ragas and talas because we think they will necessarily aid our understanding of western art music, or even western improvisation. Similarly, it is not reasonable to assume that a study of popular music will, in and of itself, make Schubert's *Lieder* more accessible.

What popular music can do is to demonstrate, perhaps more clearly than any other music, the evolution or assimilation of a particular style. This cannot be done if popular music is approached via a survey of trends. Rather, any investigation must concern itself with a methodical study of musical causes and effects. Popular music is, because of its generally accessible and frequently guileless musical content, an ideal subject for a methodological study. Lineages and influences may be traced with relative ease in popular music, and the problems of defining the salient features of a style can be dealt with more easily here than in connection with music of greater complexity and lesser familiarity. The skills acquired in such an investigation may be applied to other, perhaps more sophisticated music when experience allows. The student is not learning about the use of specific chords or melody types in order to apply that knowledge to art music. Instead, he is learning that, while style in music is a relatively fluid thing with many possible sources and influences, a methodical approach incorporating both historical and theoretical concepts can be brought to bear in such a way as to increase sensitivity to that style and the ability to perceive it.

It is no exaggeration to suggest that the perception of style is at the root of any musical study. Therefore, the study of style in popular music is relevant not only to ethnomusicology, but to any area where the refinement of an investigative method is of paramount importance, e.g., music appreciation, music history, or even introductory courses in musicology.

This study of the ballad style in the early music of the Beatles is an attempt to demonstrate some of the possibilities inherent in the investigation of popular music and, in particular, its ability to assimilate various influences and styles.

When the Beatles came out with their first single, "Love Me Do," in November 1962, it must have been difficult to determine exactly what sort of group they were. The Lennon-McCartney composition "Love Me Do" resembled nothing on the English or American pop charts of the period in its apparent disregard for the conventions of pop or rock melody, its preoccupation with perfect intervals in the two vocal parts, and its slightly blues-influenced and distinctly non-virtuoso harmonica solos. This song may well have derived from the country and western ballad style of 50s rockabilly singer Carl Perkins and resembles his "I'm Sure to Fall" in melodic conception, rhythm, and textural devices as shown by an early Beatles' recording of the song. In this version of "I'm Sure to Fall," based closely on the original, the melodic phrasing and use of parallel perfect intervals in the vocal parts in particular point to the Beatles' later "Love Me Do."

After this rather ambiguous beginning, it soon became clear that the Beatles were destined to be successful hit-makers in three reasonably distinct styles. The first of these was the pop-rock style. The Beatles' first several hits demonstrated this style, a combination of tuneful melody of distinctive contour and an energetic, uptempo rhythmic accompaniment characteristic of the more improvisatory rock styles since the mid-1950s. This style can be heard in the Beatles' second single (the first to reach the number one position in England), a song heavily influenced by the vocal sonorities of the American duo, the Everly Brothers, entitled "Please Please Me." This Lennon-McCartney composition features a vocal style in which the strongly directional melody is juxtaposed with a reiteration of the tonic, a gesture recalling the 1961 Everly Brothers' hit "Cathy's Clown."

Ex. 1. Please Please Me
(A section)

The second of the Beatles' three early styles is the rhythm and blues-rock style. This style combines the fragmented melodic style of the blues tradition (including the flatted thirds and sevenths associated with that idiom) with the limited harmonic variety of the traditional blues progression. The Beatles recorded relatively few original compositions in this style (none of the Beatles' early compositions follows the blues progression exactly), but an early American single, "I Saw Her Standing There," may, with its insistence on the tonic and flat seventh scale degrees and its blues-like harmony, be taken as representative of the type.

Ex. 2. I Saw Her Standing There
(A section)

The third of the three early styles is the slow or medium tempo ballad. It must be noted here that the term "ballad" is not, in this case, meant to imply any connection with the traditional western folk repertoire nor to suggest the presence of narrative text content. Rather, the term is used here to denote those songs exhibiting a more sustained and lyrical melodic approach in combination with a comparatively slow tempo. This type is encountered in the Beatles' original repertoire almost from the beginning. The B side of the Beatles' first single, "P.S. I Love You," demonstrates in embryonic form some of the conjunct parallel progressions and augmented chords which are to mark most of the Beatles' early ballads. This type of ballad is fully and consistently realized for the first time in "Do You Want to Know a Secret?," a 1963 Lennon composition. This song appears to be modelled harmonically after Tony Sheridan's "Why?," recorded in Hamburg, Germany, at a 1961 session for which the Beatles provided some background accompaniments.

Ex. 3. Do You Want To Know A Secret?
(A section)

Not only are the harmonic progressions and melodic rhythms comparable for the first few measures, but the arrangements of the background vocal harmonies also show a definite resemblance.

This archetypal ballad style is followed in a number of other ballads in this period. "If I Fell" contains an A section which makes conspicuous use of a conjunct progression featuring the mediant chord, and "Ask Me Why" consists harmonically of a slight re-shuffling of the same conjunct progression which characterizes Sheridan's "Why?" and Lennon's "Do You Want to Know a Secret?"

The emphasis on the mediant chord, conjunct chord progressions, or even the chromatically descending harmonies of "Secret" were not, of course, the exclusive property of either Sheridan or the Beatles. Several rock ballads of the 50s (and earlier) had made conspicuous use of similar harmonic devices, most notably "I'm Mr. Blue," "Blue Velvet," and "You Belong to Me." The conjunct chord progression (and attendant melodic options) had not been restricted to early rock ballads, however. Meredith Willson's "Till There Was You," a song recorded by the Beatles on their earliest album, prominently features such a progression. Nevertheless, the degree to which these Beatle ballads exhibit a homogeneous melodic-harmonic content must be considered unique, even though the homogeneity frequently extends only to the first section of the songs.

Along with these generally lyrical ballads, the Beatles also composed and recorded in a ballad style which may be described as an "uptown" rhythm and blues style.[1] The "uptown" style, as manifest in the work of black groups such as Smokey Robinson and the Miracles and the Shirelles, demonstrated a preference for dramatically placed minor chords (usually within the context of a major key) and a call and response vocal interaction, as well as a generally more serious and accusing tone. Although the uptown ballad style, heard, for example, in the Beatles' "No Reply," disappeared from their repertoire by late 1964, the style is important in connection with the emerging tendency of the Beatles to develop a personal synthesis of pre-existing styles. Beginning in 1964, the Beatles recorded a number of compositions which clearly demonstrate melodic-harmonic characteristics of both the rhythm and blues-rock style and the uptown rhythm and blues style. These contrasting styles can be seen in the Beatles' sixth single, "Can't Buy Me Love," which exhibits the melodic-harmonic style of the rhythm and blues style in the A section, while relying heavily on the minor mediant and submediant chords so characteristic of the uptown style in the bridge section.

Despite the fact that the Beatles had, by late 1964, proven themselves to be versatile composers and performers capable of drawing upon or synthesizing any number of different styles, there is no doubt but that the world of pop music was caught very much off-guard by the appearance of the Beatles' "Yesterday." It is probable that "Yesterday," first released as part of the British *Help!* album in 1965, was considered unique more for its accompanying string quartet than for its melodic-harmonic content. Although the use of strings per se was not an unusual gesture in rock music, the pseudo-Classical style used by the quartet in "Yesterday" was authentically innovative.

Still, the melodic-harmonic style of McCartney's "Yesterday" must also have been perceived by most listeners as demonstrative of a break in the Beatles' style. While McCartney's earlier ballad "And I Love Her" had exhibited an unusual use of nonharmonic tones and minor seventh chords, and more recent ballads had displayed a higher-than-usual number of augmented chords and an occasional major seventh chord, the majority of early Beatle ballads had remained securely within the stylistic parameters of the earlier rock and roll ballad as represented by Sheridan's "Why?" "Yesterday" seemed to represent the first major departure from this style in its conspicuous use of sustained nonharmonic tones and minor seventh chords. With "Yesterday," the Beatles appear to have moved into the world of the sophisticated adult commercial ballad, a fact substantiated by the large number of adult ballad singers who recorded the song and the widespread acceptance of the song among post-teenagers.

And yet, the apparently revolutionary qualities of "Yesterday" were not, in fact, revolutionary for two reasons: first, the song retains significant rock ballad and pop-rock characteristics to an even

Ex. 4. Yesterday
(A section)

greater extent than did earlier songs such as "And I Love Her"; second, the Beatles had actually composed in this adult commercial ballad style much earlier in their career, although these works were not recorded by them.

The traditional rock ballad and pop-rock characteristics found in "Yesterday" include the prominent use of the vi-V-IV progression in the bridge (with the same chords suggested in the A section), and the flat third relationship between major chords heard in the closing measures of the A section. The first of these characteristics is particularly associated with the older rock ballad style, while the second is found to any great extent only in earlier Beatle pop-rock songs.

The apparent stylistic inconsistency of "Yesterday" should not be seen as evidence of naivete on the Beatles' part, however. The fact that this song was accepted so widely as an adult popular ballad is proof of its credentials in that style; and it seems probable that the Beatles, and McCartney in particular, were well aware of the hybrid quality of the song since the group had, three years earlier, composed works which fit the adult ballad mold much more closely. In fact, two of the Beatles' earliest ballads, both dating from 1963 or before, are remarkable for their demonstration of a mature adult commercial ballad style. The first of these, "Love of the Loved," was composed for pop ballad singer Cilla Black and exists only in a rehearsal version by the Beatles released as a bootleg record.

Ex. 5. Love of the Loved
(A section)

This song is remarkable in a number of respects. First, its harmonic variety is unusual for an early Beatle composition. While the opening tonic-mediant progression is appropriate to the rock ballad style as well as to the adult ballad style (as shown by such ballads as "Ask My [sic] Why" and "Do You Want to Know a Secret?"), the flat mediant, minor subdominant, and flat submediant chords which follow clearly distinguish the song from the commercially released original ballads as well as from the somewhat simplistic pop-rock hits of 1963 and 1964. These varied and relatively sophisticated harmonies, found in both sections of the song, clearly belong more to an older ballad tradition (as exemplified by such songs as "We'll Be Together Again" and "Blue Moon") as does the extensive, near-sequential repetition of melodic motives also found in both sections.

A second and equally remarkable example of the adult commercial style in the Beatles' early ballads is found in "It's for You," also composed for Cilla Black in 1963. The first section of "It's for You" features prominent major and minor seventh sonorities within a harmonic progression generated by a descending bass line, a device which is to become extremely important in Beatle songs composed three or four years later, and which is also encountered in Scott's "A Taste of Honey," an adult commercial ballad recorded by the Beatles on their first British album.

Ex. 6. It's for You
(A section)

The bridge of "It's for You" is of equal interest. It exhibits a repeating "jazz waltz" rhythm combined with prominent minor added sixth, minor seventh, and diminished harmonies, and an expanding melodic motive. Once again, the song recalls the sophisticated adult ballad to a far greater extent than it does the more or less stereotyped rock ballads which the Beatles chose to record for the first three years of their career.

Nevertheless, the appearance of this relatively sophisticated style in the Beatles' early work is not as remarkable as one might suppose judging from the group's original recorded repertoire. In fact, the Beatles' experience with this style is not restricted to the recording of two musical comedy tunes on their earliest albums but dates back to the group's earliest stages. In a 1959 letter to a local journalist, McCartney states that the group "derives a great deal of pleasure from re-arranging old favourites ('Ain't She Sweet,' 'You Were Meant for Me,' 'Home,' 'Moonglow,' 'You Are My Sunshine' and others)."[2]

Of these examples, only "Moonglow," with its chromatic harmonies, actually qualifies as an adult commercial ballad; but the Beatles had relied on other commercial ballads for their subsequent recording auditions including "Besame Mucho," and "Red Sails in the Sunset" as well as "Till There Was You."

The Beatles apparent enthusiasm for the older and somewhat more sophisticated ballads is generally attributed to two factors. First, the Beatles' early skiffle phase had taught them the advantages of adapting songs of various types to their own style. Second, adult influence may well have played a major role in the Beatles' early repertoire. Paul's father had led a dance band in the 1920s and it is possible that Jim McCartney's commercial tastes were passed on to his son. Paul was, in fact, the featured vocalist on all of the Beatles' early efforts in the commercial style, a probable indication of his personal enthusiasm. Two other adults were in an even more influential position in respect to the Beatles' repertoire. According to Beatle biographer Hunter Davies, both manager Brian Epstein and producer George Martin encouraged the Beatles to perform the older ballads despite the fact that the Beatles' local reputation had been based on a more dynamic approach to traditional rock and roll.[3]

While the Beatles' early influences offer a possible explanation for their occasional adoption of the commercial ballad style, they do not explain why the Beatles should reserve their own rather unique compositions in that style for other performers, while recording themselves only those original ballads which tend to more closely fit the formulas of the traditional rock ballad.

The reasons for this unusual situation cannot be stated with certainty but two factors may be involved. Although the Beatles, in the early stages of their recording career, were in no position to ignore the counsel of their adult advisors, there is no question but that the members of the group shared a distaste for the slick ballad style of the then popular British singer Cliff Richard. While the Beatles apparently felt that the recording of commercial ballads such as "Till There Was You" and "A Taste of Honey" demonstrated their versatility, it is possible that the group made a conscious effort to shun the slicker style in their recordings of original material in order to avoid the almost inevitable comparison with Richard.

A second and perhaps more significant factor involves a conscious decision on the Beatles' part to incorporate only the simplest devices of melody and harmony in the early recordings. While the more typical rock ballads such as "Ask Me Why" and "Do You Want to Know a Secret?" are not completely devoid of stylistic surprises (the Beatles also having vowed to eliminate overworn cliches in this period[4]), the songs are clearly not equal in sophistication to the adult commercial ballads "Love of the Loved," "It's for You," and the later "Yesterday." The Beatles actually seem to have experienced a mild identity crisis in connection with the complexity of their compositions. Writing in his 1964 biography *The True Story of the Beatles*, Billy Shepherd states:

> At one time, the pair were afraid they were losing their touch as songwriters. This was because they became too obsessed with chord content. They put too much into each melody and when it came to running through the finished product, they realized it was much too complicated to catch on with the fans. It took a long time for them to realize where they were going wrong. Then they agreed: "We go for simplicity in the future. Let's stop kidding ourselves that we're great musical composers. Let's just get the sort of material that we like to sing and then stick them into the programmes."[5]

Shepherd also quotes Lennon on the subject of complexity:

> "Sometimes we strayed outside the bounds of the simple stuff — and we worried about it. For instance, 'From Me to You' was a bit on the complicated side. Actually, we both thought it would never catch on with the fans, and I think it was Paul's dad who persuaded us that it was a nice little tune . . . . "[6]

An unusual awareness of audience expectations is implicit in the Beatles' attitude at this point. The relatively slick and complex adult commercial ballads were appropriate only for nightclub singers such as Cilla Black who drew upon a wider range of ages for their following, while the Beatles could expect continued success only if it were clear that their songs were directed specifically at the teenage fans who first embraced them. It was not until the Beatles were solidly launched on their most successful career that they allowed their more sophisticated efforts to become closely identified with the group as a performing entity. Their continued popularity after 1965 suggests that their decision to publicly expand their resources was a wise one even though there have been, and will probably continue to be, critics who assert that it was the early, supposedly naive Beatles who made the greatest contribution to popular music.

NOTES

[1] This term is taken from Charlie Gillett's *The Sound of the City: The Rise of Rock and Roll* (New York: Outerbridge & Dienstrey, 1970).

[2] Hunter Davies, *The Beatles: The Authorized Biography* (New York: Dell Publishing Co., Inc., 1968), p. 69.

[3] Ibid., p. 149.

[4] Jonathan Cott, "John Lennon" in *The Rolling Stone Interviews*, Paperback Library Edition (New York: Coronet Communications, Inc., 1971), p. 199.

[5] Billy Shepherd, *The True Story of the Beatles* (New York: Bantam Books, Inc., 1964), p. 78.

[6] Ibid., p. 79.

DISCOGRAPHY

In Alphabetical Order (Performers in parenthesis)

Can't Buy Me Love (The Beatles) on *A Hard Day's Night*, United Artists UAS 3366A

Cathy's Clown (The Everly Brothers), Warner Bros. 7110

Do You Want to Know a Secret? (The Beatles) on *The Early Beatles*, Capitol ST 2309

If I Fell (The Beatles) on *A Hard Day's Night*, United Artists UAS 3366A

I'm Sure to Fall (The Beatles) on *Yellow Matter Custard*, Trademark of Quality TMQ 71032

I Saw Her Standing There (The Beatles) on *Meet the Beatles*, Capitol ST 2047

It's for You (Cilla Black), Capitol 5428

Love Me Do (The Beatles) on *The Early Beatles*, Capitol ST 2309

Love of the Loved (The Beatles) on *The Beatles: L.S. Bumblebee*, Contraband (matrix) 3626

No Reply (The Beatles) on *Beatles '65*, Capitol ST 2228

Please Please Me (The Beatles) on *The Early Beatles*, Capitol ST 2309

P.S. I Love You (The Beatles) on *The Early Beatles*, Capitol ST 2309

A Taste of Honey (The Beatles) on *The Early Beatles*, Capitol ST 2309

Till There Was You (The Beatles) on *Meet the Beatles*, Capitol ST 2047

Why? (Tony Sheridan) on *In the Beginning: The Beatles (Circa 1960)*, Polydor Stereo 244504

Yesterday (The Beatles) on *"Yesterday" . . . and Today*, Capitol ST 2553

Introduction to
HIGH-BROWS VS NO-BROWS

In 1965, Reverend David A. Noebel, Dean of the Christian Crusade Anti-Communist Youth University, went on a speaking tour to convince Americans that the Beatles were a dangerous arm of the communist plot. His short treatise *Communism, Hypnotism and the Beatles* (Christian Crusade, 1965) explained the syncopated rhythms of rock-and-roll music as they contributed to the "communist master music plan" to "make our children mentally sick." Classical music critic Abram Chasins, in "High-Brows vs No-Brows," argues that an interest in the Beatles is likely to turn a child into a music lover rather than a frenzied maniac or a communist puppet, as suggested by Rev. Noebel.

HIGH-BROWS VS NO-BROWS

by Abram Chasins

"If you can't fight 'em, join 'em." Fully ten years ago, I offered this homespun advice to dismayed friends whose children were shrieking and clutching at Elvis Presley. Those who had determined that it was time to assert parental authority had found themselves embroiled in a bitter struggle. The more they objected, the more they encountered hysteria and defiance. Others had passively let the mania run its course — a few in nostalgic remembrance of their own generation's idolatry of Vallee, Crosby and Sinatra; most in tight-lipped resignation that this, too, shall pass.

It did, of course; but only to recur in more frenzied forms, hitting a new high in Beatlemania, today's teen-age trauma. Up to a point, it is a familiar phenomenon, which should remind us that there is nothing completely new under the sun and that, without our lifting a finger, it will fade into oblivion. In its unprecedented duration and degree of intensity, however, Beatlemania is far more than an outburst of common hero worship. Despite its power to provoke bedlam and broken limbs, it is also a phenomenon we could channel constructively to reaffirm the home as a source of standards and behavior.

Surveys of how parents are coping with their children's "acting up and dressing down" have revealed that the largest number claims to be waging militant opposition to the craze, yet admits "no success" or "some success at the cost of family harmony." The next largest group claims to be "relaxing against it," supporting this position behind explanations such as "It's just adolescence" or "They're just conforming."

Anthropologists tell us that the frenzied reaction to rock-'n'-roll rhythms is a throwback to the aboriginal response to the jungle beat of the tom-tom. Where do we go from there? Barbaric rhythm is also the chief characteristic of most contemporary music, including the greatest classical masterpiece of our century, Stravinsky's "The Rite of Spring." Evidently, the mature and cultured segments of our

91

society also feel the need for a primitive outlet.

Psychologists and psychiatrists tell us that Beatlemania serves as a revolt against parental authority. Other studies conclude that the outward hysteria of Beatlemania is an antidote for the inner hysteria of "emancipated" youngsters plagued by the uncertainties of a turbulent world; and that the mass conformism provides status, safety in numbers, and a chance to let off steam in a society that suppresses instinct and emotion. Still another theory is that Beatlemania offers youngsters a chance to "find themselves" by losing themselves in self-identification with those successful and attractive "good-bad boys."

Whether or not these theories are correct, I am not qualified to judge. Music is my beat, and it is the music the Beatles compose and perform that accounts substantially for their immense fame and following.

In this area, music analysts have shown an unwillingness to recognize the extent to which popular music has been a revealing reflection of the emotions of the majority of Americans throughout our history. From the patriotic and political songs of Revolutionary days to the rock 'n' roll that has ridiculed traditions and flouted our conventions, popular songs have candidly, though often obviously, mirrored our ever-changing modes of life.

The music of the Beatles is not strictly rock 'n' roll, but a synthesis in which it is merely an element. The melodies are mongrels of cowboy and calypso traits, echoes of Anglo-Saxon folklore, all with a northern British accent. The instant appeal of the songs is rooted in the spectacular resurgence of folk singing and dancing. The harmonies are basically orthodox, with unexpected deviations and turns in the modern manner. The rhythm is a lustier and more syncopated Big Beat. Most interesting is the spicy variety of the Beatles' style, from tender ballads to tough twists.

Instrumentally, Ringo handles his drums with all the subtlety of a woodsman felling an oak, while the others slash chords across electric guitars, carefully avoiding anything complicated, as they are obliged to because of their technical limitations. Vocally, they are youthfully hoarse, and their untidy enunciation of corny lyrics is amusingly calculated to satirize our hillbillies.

As they sing and sway, they disclose revealing dualities. They are sophisticated yet disarmingly simple; their material is a composite of cliches, imaginatively woven into a texture of individual sound and style. Especially significant is the sharp intelligence with which the Beatles reverse roles with audiences and, at that point, also act as accompanists to ecstatic fans, whom they shrewdly encourage to jump, shriek and share the show in uninhibited self-expression.

Now, what's behind all this? What can we learn from the Beatles' ability to convert children's pent-up emotions into mutual love and musical enthusiasm? What needs are they fulfilling that we are not?

In an effort to answer such questions, I asked teen-agers from different localities and different backgrounds how they felt about the Beatles. Their answers made them one. In fact, with the exception of a handful of deviationists, the responses were so startlingly similar that they can be quoted collectively.

"They're adorable, they're young, they're a little kooky like us, and they're in our corner," the girls murmured dreamily. "When we wave, they wave back, and they don't tell us to shut up or dress up. Whatever we do is okay with them. They understand."

"They've got rhythm and a terrific beat," the boys said. "Their music is different, but you can get it and it gets you. They make you want to do what they do. They give us the right kind of a 'fix' — they fix it so that singing and playing aren't sissy. Belive me, when you can handle a song and a guitar, it sure rates with the girls."

Both girls and boys said, "At home, when I play my music, my folks give me a dirty look and walk out. So when they play their music, opera and classical stuff, I walk out."

"My music." "Their music." Where did they get that? They got it in homes where music, if it existed at all, was never an experience the whole family enjoyed together. They got it from parents who divide music into "good" and "bad," who still haven't learned that the more you love music, the more music you love.

The most illuminating single answer came from a youngster of fourteen. "My parents are driving me nuts," he said. "Anything I do that puts me 'in' with my gang, puts me 'out' with them. My mother made me take piano lessons. After a while, I hated music and I wouldn't practice and I got bawled out. Now I love the guitar, and I formed a combo of kids. I double at the piano, and we're the only ones who have a piano, so I asked the kids up one night to practice, and it was awful. My father put his hands over his ears and ran out of the room. My mother tried to be nice, but you could see she wasn't with it, and when we began to get real hopped up from playing together, she looked scared. When I went to Carnegie Hall to hear the Beatles, she made me feel like I was a delinquent."

I decided to start my poll of parents with this mother. I pointed out that the Beatles seem to have succeeded precisely where she had failed — in making music a rich and joyful part of her boy's life. Further, that going to Carnegie Hall is the beginning of a good habit. I then asked her whether she wouldn't rather have her son making music with his friends at home, even if it was noisy, than not to know what he was doing.

"I'm amazed at you," she answered. "With your standards, how can you think of this in terms of music? It's just childish, cheap stuff. We made every sacrifice to give Billy lessons, so that he would know the difference between this maudlin trash and great music. He resisted it, all of it."

That's where she was wrong. That's not what Billy resisted. What he did resist, and rightly so, was the whole senseless paraphernalia of making music in a vacuum, the isolated drudgery of practicing an instrument not of his own choosing and before he had any desire for music. As for the "cheap stuff" that had inspired Billy not only to love music, but to read it and practice without pressure in order to participate in it — indeed I call it music, for the ingredients are essentially the same as those that exist in music of more permanent value.

Another parent said, "The Beatle craze? Rebellious enthusiasm, that's what it is. The madder I get, the more satisfaction my children get from swooning over that junk."

"Rebellious enthusiasm." Take away the adjective, and enthusiasm remains — the most precious of all qualities that bring meaning and joy to our lives. Haven't we all been sick at heart over our children's apathy and blase boredom? The Beatles have given them something to get excited about. We could be more grateful and far more alert to the implications of what they have done.

The parents of the boy who brought his combo home should have realized that, in his enthusiasm, he was trying to include them in this important part of his life. He was paying them the highest compliment possible, trusting them and their reactions in front of his friends. They should have been proud of the good job they had done, up to that point. Then they misbehaved, like children. Equally immature was the attitude of the mother whose untimely emphasis on standards had all but destroyed her boy's innate musicality.

Don't worry about standards; just set them yourself. They're contagious. Children's tastes are always changing, anyway. I remember a battle in our family over my thirteen-year-old cousin, who was an insatiable reader of comic books. Today, he is one of the most literate men I know. Why not? He got the habit of reading.

One parent to whom I told this said, "It's not the same, if you're implying that the kids are getting the listening habit through the Beatles. How can they listen when they keep shrieking along?" Wait a minute. The kids know all the words and every note, or they couldn't join in. They must have listened, and attentively, to radio or records. As for the excellent habit of collecting records, an enormous number of children told me they started with the Beatles, whose records are now alphabetically stored between Bach and Beethoven.

If we really value the fact that our nation has become the greatest center of musical interest and activity in the world, every factor that made it so is as healthy as the others. Who cares whether a child is a music lover because Ringo's bongos are the "status cymbals" of his peers? The only thing wrong with that is our adult snobbery that excludes us and encourages them to oppose us. Won't we stimulate their affection and respect if we show that our broader interest in music has been intensified by their own interest?

Beatlemania was turned to effective account and even to the "pursuit of excellent" by the mother of the looniest little Beatlebug I know. He had been struggling valiantly but unsuccessfully with a guitar, which he played passionately and poorly. His mother listened, suffered with him, and then bought him a recording by the superb flamenco artist, Montoya. The boy played it from morning till night through an entire weekend. His mother then took him to a concert by Julian Bream and watched her son's eyes grow as big as saucers over that supreme virtuosity and ease.

The next day, the youngster was up at 5:00 a.m. slaving at his guitar. His mother had to drag him away from it to go to school. That night, he blurted out, "Could I have guitar lessons, please?" He could and did.

And it all started through those boys from Liverpool — from the fun they get and give through music, and because of their warmth, easy humor and astuteness. Their realistic and modest public statements show that they know exactly who they are, where they stand, and that their party may soon be over.

But a humdinger it surely has been and still is. The long list of honors bestowed on these sons of humble parents has now been crowned by Queen Elizabeth with the Order of the British Empire. Their earnings this year and the products named for them are expected to gross over $100 million, and the same figure applies to the number of their records sold.

All this reflects affirmation, not protestation. And we may be certain that none of us could be more pleased than those ingratiating fellows to discover that the vogue which enriched them so handsomely has also enriched their fervent little American fans, in ways that cannot be measured by money.

Introduction to
THE SECOND GOLDEN AGE OF POP

The year was 1966. On July 2, *Strangers in the Night*, by Frank Sinatra, bumped *Paperback Writer* from the number one spot on the *Billboard* chart, thus signaling the arrival of a "second golden age of pop," according to Steven Holroyd. (By the way, *Paperback Writer* was back on top on July 9.)

THE SECOND GOLDEN AGE OF POP

by Steven Holroyd

Nineteen-sixty-six probably won't go down in history as the year in which a 50-year-old singer called Frank Sinatra made No. 1 in the charts with a song which might have been written any time in the last fifty years.

Nevertheless the event has, I believe, a much deeper significance than is at first apparent.

For I have a strong impression that we are seeing the birth of a second Golden Age of popular music. Never before have songs of such high quality and prodigious variety been available to — and sought after by — so vast a public.

Tin Pan Alley's two decades of money-spinning imbecility are over. After the rash of contrived fads and crazes, overnight sensations who quickly become overnight disasters, after a surfeit of utterly inconsequential, imitative and repetitious musical trivia during a period which was rightly called "the age of the amateur," Tin Pan Alley seems to have pulled itself up by its guitar strings to produce popular music which ranks in quality with the best tunes from the first Golden Age between the wars.

The significance of Sinatra's No. 1 is that the singer and the song are both timeless in style. Good gimmicks come and go; good music lasts for ever. It has taken a little time, but gradually people in the music business have woken up to the fact that what they are selling is music — not sex-appeal, tee shirts, images, hair-styles, etc.

Where there was once fierce competition in column inches, there is now competition in producing good music, good sounds, good arrangements. Musical rubbish — and often highly successful musical rubbish — has been part of the scene for years and will always be with us. But happily the majority of Tin Pan Alley's denizens have raised their sights above pelvic level and the Top Twenty is all the better for it.

Today's music covers a far wider range of styles, sounds and sources than ever before; musical skill and arranging talent has developed out of all recognition; and the strait-jacket of the popular

99

Western song form has been decimated by some highly original and imaginative modern songwriters.

In the late forties and early fifties, before the record boom had really got under way, we were listening to dance bands, to thoroughly orthodox songs and thoroughly orthodox singers like Crosby, Sinatra, Dickie Valentine, Dennis Lotis, Guy Mitchell and so on.

But a revolution was simmering and it was sparked off by two important developments. The first was Bill Haley's rock 'n' roll sound — "Rock Around the Clock" was the first record to sell a million in Britain — which really heralded the arrival of the beat boom. Romantic songs about moon and June suddenly became about as effective as a cement parachute as far as the majority of record buyers were concerned.

The second phenomenon was the emergence of Elvis Presley who added sex-appeal to beat.

(Incidentally it is ironic to reflect that what really happened to make British music so internationally acclaimed was that it received a stimulating injection of lifeblood from American Negro music — a strong "coloured" influence is apparent in most of Britain's top singers today — yet it was really introduced to Britain by two white artists who had drawn their inspiration from the Negro idom.)

The fantastic success of rock 'n' roll unleashed a veritable army of British Presleys on an unsuspecting public and our musical output became one vast three-chord twelve-bar blues.

In impact, if not in kind, the rock 'n' roll revolution was similar to the bop revolution in jazz. While dozens of gleefully goateed bopsters jumped on the bop wagon only to find the destination board clearly marked "Obscurity," a handful, led by Charlie Parker, really broke through and contributed something of lasting value to the body of jazz music. In exactly the same way the rock 'n' roll boom left hundreds of disillusioned casualties in its wake; but it had its Charlie Parker in the shape of the Beatles.

The Beatles made it because they played good music. If they had all been bald it would scarcely have made any difference. They have become the most phenomenally successful artists in the history of entertainment because of their music. In fact (protect me from their 273 million teenage fans) they have very little else to offer as entertainers.

Like Frank Sinatra, they are good singers of good songs — and *that* is why they are world-beaters, not because they make funny quips at Press conferences, not because they come from Liverpool, not because they have been skillfully promoted.

In 1964, I wrote of the Beatles: "Their arrival means that the days of the cardboard cut-out pop singer are numbered (just count up how many have fallen by the wayside); it also means that tunes of a higher melodic quality are getting into the hit parade. In a sense, their success is a throwback to the days before records, before television, before press officers, when singers made it on their own, by going round the halls singing their own songs and capturing their audience not with echo chambers, not with phoney front page stories . . . but by their stage presence, by their sincerity and by their own natural musical gifts."

What exactly did the Beatles do?

One thing is certain — it's not a bit of good asking them. And this, in a way, is a clue to their success. They did what came naturally and were unfettered by the musical conventions which for so long had determined the structure of pop songs.

John Lennon and Paul McCartney have great gifts of melodic invention, a natural ear for harmony and an original concept of song construction which results, in part, from their complete lack of musical training.

Brilliant arrangers and orchestrators with years of training and experience behind them would give their right arms to be able to write songs like "Michelle" and "If I Fell." They just can't do it because they lack that freshness of approach. Their musical minds are corrupted by orthodoxy and commerciality. Sure they can write a nice, slick, glib and polished original — but it will never have that spark which distinguishes a great song from a professionally competent one.

The Beatles were not just one of a number of groups who came to the fore at the time of the Liverpool onslaught on Tin Pan Alley. They were THE group. They stuck predominantly to their own songs at a time when practically everybody else had their ears glued to record players churning out the latest releases of little known coloured groups.

Of course they did their share of listening and were influenced by the Everly Brothers, the Isley Brothers, Little Richard and even Elvis Presley — but they also had their own story to tell. And what a best-seller it was!

The tidal wave of the Beatles' success produced a long wake of subsidiary waves on which groups like Gerry and the Pacemakers, Billy J. Kramer, Swinging Blue Jeans, the Searchers, the Merseybeats and later the Animals and the Rolling Stones rode to fame.

Said John Lennon when talking to me about the early days: "I do resent it when people say we've done nothing to earn our success. Eppy went round for months in London trying to get people interested in us but nobody wanted to know. 'From Liverpool?' they said. 'You must be joking.' Well we got annoyed about this so we started plugging the Liverpool bit — sort of defensively. Then suddenly it started to happen and, before long, everything was Liverpool.

This means that the other Merseyside groups that came along after us didn't have the trouble we had to get accepted. I don't mind that — good luck to them."

Unfortunately so much was made of the Liverpool sound, the haircuts, the wisecracks and all the other paraphernalia without which the National Press could hardly survive, that the really exceptional quality of the Beatles' songs was overlooked.

The very first Beatle song I heard was "Love Me Do" and it caught my attention because of its unusual phrasing, its 38-bar construction and a middle-eight which, at first hearing seemed dreadfully naive — but which sort of crept up on you later.

Some time later I heard the Beatles rehearsing "She Loves You" in a Stockholm hotel room and I was surprised to hear them sing a sixth chord at the end — something I'd heard no other group do, outside the more sophisticated Four Freshmen school. On that same occasion I remember asking them why they had an eleven-bar middle in one of their tunes. Said Paul McCartney, "Have we? It just seemed to fit like that."

For a long time it was fashionable for jazz musicians to put down the Beatles as musical pretenders, fakers, phoneys, etc., etc. Certainly there was a rash of unschooled, inept, cloth-eared groups at the time of the beat boom, but only the most seething bigot would put the Beatles in this category.

Certainly, too, they are not particularly brilliant musicians — but as songwriters they are unchallenged. Ask Peggy Lee, Duke Ellington, Ella Fitzgerald, Gerry Mulligan, Keely Smith, Gary McFarland, etc., etc., etc.

One thing that characterises much of the Lennon-McCartney output — apart from their tendency to play almost everything in E (very natural for guitarists!) — is the continuity of their melodies. They seem to have an aversion to rest bars and "It Won't Be Long" provides a good example of this. The song opens with a short phrase which ends on the first beat of the third bar. If any orthodox songwriter had written this phrase it would almost certainly have been followed by three crochet rests and a bar tacit to make it into a four-bar section. But the Beatles make it a three-bar phrase and begin the repeat on the second beat of the fourth bar.

An even more extraordinary example of their indifference to the conventions of song construction is provided by "I'll Be Back," an excellent tune divided predominantly into six-bar segments but which also includes passages of six and a half and nine and a half bars.

Jeff Muston, a former jazz trombonist, who has the job of transforming Beatle tunes into sheet music says: "As a musician I had always thought that there was nothing really original in music. Most

102

of it is derivative. But the Beatles really deserve the description 'original.' When these half-bars arise I have to write them as an odd bar of 2/4. Half-bars also occur in 'Baby's In Black' which is in 12/8 time. In some cases the tunes are so difficult to analyse that I just have to count the beats and divide by four or eight."

Another gift which puts the Beatles way out in front of their contemporaries is their ability to write rich middle eights — or, in their cases, middle elevens, fifteens, etc. So often in popular music a good idea sags because of a drab and colourless bridge. This is rarely the case with Lennon and McCartney. "I Should Have Known Better," for example, has a superb 16-bar middle which reaches a great climax of its own with a five-tone interval in the melodic line on the word "mine" — or, rather, "mi-uh-huh-ine." There are great middle sections, too, in "You Can't Do That" (a lusty dominant seventh resolving into the relative minor of the written key) and in "I Don't Want To Spoil The Party."

None of these examples is, of course, revolutionary, but they are relatively rare in the musical context in which the Beatles operate.

It is principally in their music that the Beatles excel. In the matter of writing lyrics nobody would suggest that the Beatles are in the Lorenz Hart or Noel Coward class. But even so, they have a great gift for fitting words to the tune. In "She's a Woman," for instance, there is a beautiful marriage of words and melody with the line, " . . . fooling I know she isn't." I can't explain why — just listen.

Other than that there are altogether too many diamond rings being bought, too many girls being given everything, and one unforgivable case of someone being loved "until the cows come home."

However, that is not much of a price to pay for a hundred-odd refreshingly original and compelling numbers, some of which will undoubtedly become the standards of their generation — the sort of tunes, in fact, of which our children will say to their children, "Ah, they don't write songs like that today."

103

Introduction to
LEARNING FROM THE BEATLES

What kind of knowledge can be gained from rock-and-roll songs or, specifically, from the Beatles' songs? In 1967, Richard Corliss speculated in the pages of *Commonweal* (May 12, 1967, pages 234–236) that most colleges would offer programs in rock-and-roll by the year 1977. His piece, "A Beatle Metaphysic," was, in part, a reaction to an article titled "The Aesthetics of Rock" (*Crawdaddy*, March 1967, pages 11–14+), by Richard Meltzer. Meltzer's article, later to be the basis for a book by the same title (*The Aesthetics of Rock*, Something Else Press, 1970), parodied the efforts of the intellectual community to explain rock music. Richard Poirier, in "Learning from the Beatles," ventures carefully into the subject of Meltzer's satire, announcing that he will limit his comments to the **Sergeant Pepper** LP and a few singles also released in 1967, instead of attempting "an intelligent piece on the general subject of 'rock,' " which is too broad to survey in any one essay or book.

LEARNING FROM THE BEATLES

by Richard Poirier

I am proposing that a line of force in literature beginning with some American works of the last century and passing through Eliot and Joyce to the present has offered a radical challenge to customary ways of thinking about expression in or out of the arts. And I am further proposing that because this challenge hasn't been sufficiently recognized, criticism, especially as practiced in the university, where it should be most exploratory, simply fails to give an adequate reading to some of the very texts it cares most about, and shows almost no capacity to cope with what are considered less distinguished ones placed under the heading of popular culture: in films, advertising, TV entertainment, the music of the young, or dance.

Nothing confirms the persistence of outmoded criteria and the consequent failure to account for certain new forms of expression so much as the flagrant triviality with which any of these subjects is discussed or studied. I'll content myself here with one example, rock music, and with one work, *Sgt. Pepper's Lonely Hearts Club Band*. In so restricting my attention, I mean to suggest that any study of popular culture must start with analyses that are as close, disciplined, and detailed as one can make them. The chances of doing an intelligent piece on the general subject of "rock" (and there are many bad tries every week) are about as good as doing such a piece on "the symphony" or on "the drama" — in other words, none. Opportunistic snobbery can let anyone think that an item of popular culture somehow is easier to discuss than one belonging to so-called high culture. If anything, the reverse is true, simply because there haven't yet been developed any satisfactory conventions or methods for discussing a subject like rock or even so documented and revered a subject as film, which is fast being promoted from the category of the popular into the category of the high.

When it comes to the performed arts, even in the case of dance, where it is at least possible to locate the event and the relative importance of its contributing elements, such as music and costume, criticism is more difficult than its most voluble practitioners can very well afford to realize. With rock the difficulties are compounded. Who knows just what it is? To talk mostly about the lyrics is to turn it into literature; to talk mostly about the recorded music can lead to the self-promoting technicalities of a Ned Rorem; and talk about concert appearances usually degenerates into a kind of ecstatic socio-sexual reportage. It is perhaps impossible to account for the simultaneity of effects in rock music, to describe, as criticism at some point ought to do, simply what it is like to experience a live performance of rock. It may be that it needs, more than do most other kinds of performance, to be broken up into component parts — an unfortunate possibility — before there can be intelligent discussion of any one of them.

One thing is clear in any case: the claim that the problem is generational and that what the young feel about rock can't be felt by their elders merely begs the larger question of what the phenomenon is to begin with. Nor is the generational claim at all justified by any demonstrated competence among young rock reviewers. Where there are good pieces, mostly in *Rolling Stone* magazine and *Crawdaddy*, they are only unremarkably so, and most of them display the adult vices, including a kind of Germanic fondness for categorization: the Mersey beat, the raving style, trip songs, the San Francisco school, the love sound, folk-rock, and the rock-folk-pop tradition are typical of the terms that get bandied about with desperate and charming hope.

Reviews of popular music in the major newspapers and magazines are much worse, however, and before the *Sgt. Pepper* album practically no space even for an intelligent note was given the Beatles in any of them. Once such notices did begin to appear, any adult easily victimized by a reputed generational gap need only have read reviews of *Sgt. Pepper* in the *New York Times* and the *Village Voice* by Richard Goldstein to discover that youth is no guarantee of understanding. In his early twenties, he sounded already like an ancient. Some of his questions — does the album have any real unity? — were not necessary even when originally asked some two thousand years ago; while others are a bad dream of Brooks and Warren: the "lyrical technique" of "She's Leaving Home" is "uninspired narrative, with a dearth of poetic irony." The song is in fact one of *Sgt. Pepper's* satirically funniest cuts, though someone Goldstein's age mightn't as easily see this as would someone older. Recognition of its special blend of period sentimentality and elegance of wit is conferred upon the listener not by his being chronologically young but by his having once lived with that especially English blend of tones from Beatrice Lillie or Noel Coward, and their wistful playfulness about the genteel.

It would of course be unfair to expect that rock criticism from the young should be more competent than is most criticism of other kinds from people of all ages. Indeed it shouldn't be expected to be as good. For that reason alone, however, the special difficulties of discussing rock or any other popular forms of expression should itself become a subject of intense academic study, as has been proposed for some years by Richard Hoggart and his colleagues at the Centre for Contemporary Cultural Studies at Birmingham University. Prudery in this matter is less pardonable than youthful arrogance, but it is of a piece with it.

If young would-be critics of rock think it presumptuous when literary critic-teachers of my age comment on their special field, then most academic adjudicators think so, too. They regard as a betrayal of standards any discussions of popular culture which involve the detailed scrutiny usually reserved for historically established works. Such an attitude is as frightened as it is unscholarly. It rescues itself by establishing a hierarchy of proper interests, much as does a similar attitude on the part of some literary intellectuals of the old left. The latter's fear of any enthusiastic lapse of taste, or what a representative figure like Philip Rahv disparages as "trendiness," is consistent with their fear of losing place in some social-literary-political alliance. All three factions — the youth establishment as represented by journalists of rock, the academic conservatives, and the old-left literati — while sustaining one another's illusions of status by being officially at odds, share a fearful resistance to the kind of inquiry into contemporary expression which would upset long-standing commitments to cultural priorities.

Culturally speaking, the importance of the *Sgt. Pepper* album is that it finally put the Beatles, in the summer of 1967, beyond the shabby treatment or defensive patronizations of any of these factions. It isn't enough to say that it was then the latest and most remarkable of the thirteen albums composed and performed by the Beatles since 1964; some such claim could have been made for each album when it appeared. *Sgt. Pepper* wasn't in the line of any continuous development. Rather, it was at the time a sort of eruption, an accomplishment for which no one could have been wholly prepared. It therefore substantially enlarged and modified all the work that preceded it. Those who took it this way went back to the earlier Beatles as one might to earlier Mark Twain after something as astonishingly unexpected in its brilliance as *The Adventures of Huckleberry Finn*. How did such a thing happen? The evidence can be heard: on each record which, while being unmistakably theirs, is nonetheless full of exploratory peculiarities not heard on the others; in the way the release even of a single set off a new surge of energy among their many imitators; in a self-delighting inventiveness that gradually exceeded the sheer physical capacities even of four such brilliant musicians. The consequent necessity for expanded orchestral and electronic support had reached the point where the *Sgt. Pepper* album had to be wholly, if randomly, conceived in studio with as many as forty-eight instruments. Still in their mid-twenties, they had meanwhile made two movies, *A Hard Day's Night* and *Help!*, which show some of their comic and theatrical flair; and John Lennon had written two books of verbal play that suggest why no one is ever in danger of reading too much into the lyrics of their songs.

At this point the group had so affected personal as well as musical styles that no one could any longer ignore their impact. But how to deal with it? The easiest way was, and is, to sociologize, especially since this allows the good and the bad in the popular arts to be treated equally and delays those qualitative discriminations which only the higher arts are supposed to invite. What do the Beatles "represent"? it was asked — a favorite question in the shelving process. Of course this, like any game, can be played to some profit. The Beatles show (or showed) an aspect of the youth movement unique to the generations since World War II. They are in the best sense artistocratic: in their carelessness, their assumption that they can enact anyone else's life just for the fun of it, their tolerance for the things they do make fun of, their delight in wildness along with a disdain for middle-class rectitudes, their easy expertness, their indifference to the wealth they are happy to have, their pleasures in costume and in a casual eccentricity of ordinary dress, their in-group language not meant, any more than is Bob Dylan's — another such aristocrat — to make ordinary sense. True. But one must be wary. Such characterizations, by giving the new a distinguished social label of the old, merely accommodate it, sap it of its disruptive powers. So, too, with the usual kind of cultural elevation accorded the popular arts. You know, the way jazz is like Bach? Well, sometimes the Beatles are like Monteverdi and sometimes their songs are even better than Schumann's. Liverpool boys of their sort have been let into Eton before, and not on the assumption that it would be the style of Eton that would change.

It won't be easy to accommodate the Beatles, and that's nowadays almost the precondition for exciting the pastoral concern of Responsible Critics. Literary and academic grown-ups will discover that their favorite captive audience, the young in school, really have listened to the Beatles' kind of music and won't buy the yarn of significance that ensnares most adult talk about the other arts. Any effort to account for what the Beatles are doing will be difficult, as I've learned from this inexpert and not very extensive try, but only to the extent that talking about the experience of any work of art is more difficult than talking about the theory of it, or the issues in it, or the history around it. The results of any such effort by a number of people would be of importance not just for popular music but for all the arts. People who listen to the Beatles love them — what about that? Why isn't there more talk about pleasure, about the excitement of witnessing a performance, about the excitement that goes into a performance of any kind? Such talk could set in motion a radical and acutely necessary amendment to the literary and academic club rules. Since the exalted arts (to which the novel, about a century ago, was the last genre to be admitted) have all but surrendered the provision of fun and entertainment to the popular arts, criticism must turn to film and song if it is to remind itself that the arts really do not need to be boring, no matter how much copy can be made from the elaboration of current theories of boredom.

Critical confrontations initiated in this spirit could give a new status to an increasingly unfashionable kind of criticism: to close-up, detailed concern for performance, for enactment and execution in a work of art. Film and song, the two activities in which young people are now especially interested, and about which they are learning to talk fairly well, may yield something to other kinds of scrutiny, but they yield much more to this kind. So does literature, on the very infrequent occasions when it is so treated. The need is for intense localization of interest and a consequent modesty of description, in the manner of Stark Young's dramatic criticism, or Bernard Haggin's writing about classical music and jazz, or Edwin Denby and, more recently, Robert Garis on ballet. Imagining an audience for such criticism, the critic thinks not of a public with Issues and Topics at the ready, but rather of a group of like-minded people who find pleasure in certain intensive acts of looking and listening. Looking and listening to something with such a group, imaginary or real, means checking out responses, pointing to particular features, asking detailed questions, sharing momentary excitements. People tend to listen to recordings of the Beatles the way families in the last century listened to readings of Dickens, and it might be remembered by literary snobs that the novel then, like the Beatles and even film now, was considered a popular form of entertainment generally beneath serious criticism, and most certainly beneath academic attention.

The Beatles' music is said to belong to the young, but if it does that's only because the young have the right motive for caring about it — they enjoy themselves. They also know what produces the fun they have, by phrase and instrument, or sometimes by sheer volume, and they're very quick, as I've discovered, to shoot down inflated interpretations. They should indeed exercise proprietary rights. This is the first time that people of school age have been tuned in to sounds invented not by composers approved by adults but in to sounds invented by their own near contemporaries, sounds associated with lyrics, manners, and dress that they also identify as their own. David Amram, the New York Philharmonic's first resident composer, is understandably optimistic that this kind of identification will develop an avidity of attention to music that could be the salvation of American musical composition and performance.

Perhaps in some such way the popular arts can help restore all the arts to their status as entertainment and performance. To help this process along it isn't necessary that literary and academic grown-ups go to school to their children. Rather, they must begin to ask some childlike and therefore some extremely difficult questions about particular works: Is this any fun? How and where is it any fun? And if it isn't, why bother? While listening together to recordings of popular music, people of any age tend naturally to ask these questions, and I've heard them asked by young people with an eager precision which they almost never exhibit, for want of academic encouragement, when they talk about a poem or a story. If, as I've suggested, their writing about music isn't nearly so good as their talk can be, this may only mean that the conventions of written criticism serve rock even less well than they do the other arts.

In proposing that a developed appreciation of the popular arts can redirect and enhance an appreciation of all the arts, I am not suggesting that the only way lies in some unhistorical and unlearned close attentiveness to aspects of performance. An artist performs with the materials at hand, and these include whatever accents, phrases, images have gotten into one's head or voice, ears, or eyes. This poses, as we've seen, a problem of *self*-expression and "sincerity." It also offers an enormous opportunity to certain artists who feel challenged by it. Such artists tend, as in the examples of Joyce, Eliot, and others discussed in earlier chapters, to be unusually allusive both in their direct references and in their styles. They aren't sure — and in this they are classical and Johnsonian in tendency — that anything in their modes of expression really belongs to them. The *Sgt. Pepper* album is an example of how these same tendencies are at work in areas of the popular arts and are perhaps indigenous to the best art of any kind now being performed.

Nearly all the songs of the *Sgt. Pepper* album and on the two singles that followed it — "All You Need Is Love" and "Baby, You're a Rich Man" — are in fact quite broadly allusive: to the blues, to jazz hits of the thirties and forties, to classical music, early rock and roll, previous cuts by the Beatles themselves. Much of the comedy in these songs, and much of their historical resonance, as in the stately Wagnerian episode in "A Day in the Life," is managed in this way. Mixing of styles and tones reminds the listener that one kind of feeling about a subject isn't enough, and that any single induced

112

feeling must often exist within the context of seemingly contra-dictory alternatives. Most good groups offer something of this kind, like the Who, with the brilliant drummer Keith Moon. In songs like "Don't Look Away" and "So Sad About Us," Moon, working with the composer-guitarist Pete Townsend, calls forth a complicated response in a manner nicely described in *Crawdaddy* by Jon Landau, one of the best rock reviewers: "Townsend scratches his chorus, muf-fles his strings, or lets the chord stand out full depending on what Moon is doing — the result being a perfectly unified guitar-drum sound that can't help but make you feel happy even while the lyrics tell you to feel sad."

The Beatles often work for similar mixtures, but with an addi-tional nuance: especially in later songs, one of the interwoven strands is likely to be an echo of some familiar, probably cliched musical, verbal, or dramatic formula. These echoes, like the soap-opera back-ground music of "She's Leaving Home" or the jaunty music-hall tones of "When I'm Sixty-four," have the enriching effect that allusiveness can bring to poetry: of expanding a situation toward the simultaneous condition of pathos, because the situation is seen as recurrent and therefore possibly insoluble, and comic, because the recurrence has finally passed into cliche.

Any close listening to musical groups soon establishes the fact that as composers and performers the Beatles repay attention prob-ably more than does any other group, American or English. They offer something for nearly everyone and respond to almost any kind of interest. The Rolling Stones, by some considered the greatest rock performers, don't, I think, have the range of musical familiarity that prods the inventiveness of Lennon, or McCartney, or their producer George Martin, whose contributions of electronic and orchestral no-tation really made him one of the Beatles, particularly when their performances moved exclusively into studio. Only Dylan shows something equivalent to the Beatles in his combination of talents as composer, lyricist, and performer, along with his capacity to carry within him the history of country and rock and roll music.

In performance the Beatles exhibit — I write in the present tense because I'm referring to films and recordings — a nearly total theatri-cal power. It is a power so unencumbered and so freely diverse both for the group and for each of its members as to create an element of suspense attributable only to the greatest theatrical performers: an expectation that this time there really will be a failure of good taste. They never wholly lose themselves in anyone else's styling, however, or in their own exuberance; they never succumb to the excitements they generate, much less those of their audience. It's unthinkable that they would lend themselves for the rock and wreck sequence of the Yardbirds in Antonioni's *Blow-up*. That particular

113

performance, quite aside from what it contributed to a brilliant film, is a symptom of the infiltration even into popular music of the decadence by which entertainment is being displaced by a self-abasing enactment of what is implicit in the *form* of entertainment — in this instance, of group playing that gives way to animosities and a destructive retaliation against recalcitrant instrumental support.

When the Beatles sound as if they are heading orchestrally into self-obliterating noise, it is very often only that they may assert their presence vocally in quite the opposite direction: by contrasting choir-boy cooing, by filigrees of voice-play coming from each of them, as in the reprise of *Sgt. Pepper*, for instance, or, as in "Lovely Rita," the little choral oo's and masturbatory gaspings — all of these suggesting, in their relation to solo, crosscurrents of feeling within an agreed area of play. Manners so instinctively free and yet so harmonious could not be guided from outside, either by an audience or even by directorial pointers, however much the latter did help in rescuing them from a boyish enslavement to Elvis Presley, an otherwise indispensable influence, in their first, hard-to-find recording of 1961 made in Hamburg with Ringo's predecessor at the drums, Peter Best.

As is the taste of all great performers — in athletics, in politics, in any of the arts — the taste of the Beatles or of Dylan is an emanation of personality, of a self that is the generous master but never the creature of its audience. Taste in such instances is inseparable from a stubbornness of selfhood, and it doesn't matter that the self has been invented for the theater. Any self is invented as soon as any purpose is conceived. But the Beatles are a special case in not being *a* self at all. They are a group, and the unmistakable group identity exists almost in spite of sharp individuation, each of them, except the now dead Martin,* known to be unique in some shaggy way. There are few other groups in which even one or two of the members are as publicly recognizable as any of the Beatles, and this can't be explained as a difference simply in public relations. It is precisely this unusual individuation which explains, I think, why the Beatles are so much stronger than any other group and why they don't need, like the Who, to play at animosities on stage. The pretense doesn't communicate the presence of individual Who but rather an anxiety at their not instinctively feeling like individuals when they are together.

The Beatles, on the other hand, enhance the individuality of one another by the sheer elaborateness by which they arrive at a cohesive sound and by a musical awareness of one another that isn't

---

Editor's note: Poirier's reference to "the now dead Martin" is unclear. Perhaps he has confused producer George Martin with manager Brian Epstein, who died in 1967.

distinguishable from the multiple directions allowed in the attainment of harmony. Like members of a great athletic team, like such partners in dance as Nureyev and Fonteyn, or like some jazz combos, the Beatles in performance seem to draw their aspirations and their energy not from the audience but from one another. Their close, loyal, and affectionate personal ties are of course not irrelevant, and the evident pain of McCartney's departure, having something to do with the, to him, intrusion into the group of Yoko Ono, Lennon's wife, merely confirms one's sense of the intense emotional interrelationship of the four of them.

The incentive for what they accomplish seems to be sequestered among them, a tensed responsiveness that encourages from Harrison, as in "And Your Bird Can Sing," what sounds like the best guitar playing in the world and which provokes the immense productivity of Lennon and McCartney. The amount they have composed might be explained by commercial venture but not the daring and originality of each new single or album. Of course the promise of "new sounds" is itself a commercial necessity in their business, as the anxieties of, say, the second album of the Jefferson Airplane indicated, but the Beatles are reported to have enough unreleased songs for still other albums, and it's not merely "new sounds" that they produce, an easy enough matter with orchestral support, electronics and Asiatic importations. They produce different *styles*, different musical conceptions and revisions of sentiment that give an unprecedented variety to an artistic career that had its proper beginning a mere four or five years before *Sgt. Pepper*. The freshness of each effort is often so radically different from the one before, as any comparison among *Rubber Soul, Revolver*, and *Sgt. Pepper* will indicate, as to constitute risk rather than financial ambition – especially three such albums, along with a collection of earlier songs, *Yesterday and Today*, in a period just over eighteen months.

They are the ones who get tired of the sounds they have made, and the testings and teasings that produce each new album are self-inflicted. If they are careerist it is in the manner not of the late Judy Garland, reminding us in each concert of "Somewhere Over the Rainbow" and the pains of show biz, but of John Coltrane who, when he died in 1967 at forty, was also about to give up performance in public altogether, even though his reputation as one of the most influential musicians in jazz and its greatest saxophonist guaranteed him an increasingly profitable concert career. His interest in music was a continually inventive one, an effort to broaden the possibilities, as the Beatles did in studio, of his music and his instruments. Like Harrison with his guitar, he managed with the soprano sax to produce a nearly Oriental sound, and this discovery led him to an interest in Indian music much as Harrison was led to the study of the sitar. And again like the Beatles, Coltrane's experimentation was the more intense because he and his sidemen, Elvin Jones and McCoy Tyner, achieved a remarkable degree of liberating, energizing empathy.

Almost all such champions are extraordinary and private men who work with an audience, as the phrase goes, only when that audience is composed of the few who can perform with them. Otherwise, the audience is what it ought to be: not participants, as John Cage and the Becks of The Living Theatre would have it, but witnesses or listeners to a performance. The audience who in the theme song of *Sgt. Pepper* is so "lovely" that "we'd like to take you home with us" is a wholly imaginary one, especially on a record contrived as an escape from public performance.

More aloof from politics than the Stones, their topicality is of music, the social predicaments, and especially the sentiments traditional to folksongs and ballads. Maybe the most important service of the Beatles and similar groups is the restoration to good standing of the simplicities that have frightened us into irony and the search for irony; they locate the beauty and pathos of commonplace feelings even while they work havoc with fashionable or tiresome expressions of those feelings. A particularly brilliant example is the record, released some weeks after the *Sgt. Pepper* album, with "Baby, You're a Rich Man" on one side and "All You Need Is Love" on the other. "Baby, You're a Rich Man" opens with an inquiry addressed by McCartney and Harrison to Lennon, who can be said to represent here a starry-eyed fan's version of the Beatles themselves: "How does it feel to be / One of the beautiful people?" This and subsequent questions are asked of the "rich man" in a reverentially high but devastatingly lilting voice, to the accompaniment of bursts of sitar music and the clip-clopping of Indian song. The sitar, an instrument Harrison studied in India for six weeks with Ravi Shankar ("George," he reported, "was truly humble"), here suggests not the India of "Within You, Without You" evoked on the *Sgt. Pepper* album, the India of the Bhagavad-Gita. It is rather another India, of fabulous riches, the India of the British and their Maharajahs, a place for exotic travel, but also for josh sticks and the otherworldliness of a "trip." All these possibilities are at work in the interplay of music and lyrics. Contributing to the merely social and satiric implications of the song, the Indian sounds operate in the manner of classical allusion in Pope: they expand to the ridiculous the cant of jet-set, international gossip columns — "one of the beautiful people" or "baby, you're a rich man now" or "how often have been been there?" But, as in Pope, the instrument of ridicule here, the sitar, is allowed in the very process to remain unsullied and eloquent.

The social implications of the song carry more than a hint of self-parody, since the comic mixtures of verbal and musical phrasing refer us to similar mixtures that are a result of the Beatles' fantastic fortune: Liverpool boys, still in their twenties, once relatively poor and now enormously rich, once socially nowhere and now internationally "there," once close to home both in fact and in their music but now implicated not only in the Mersey beat but in the Ganges sound, in travel to India and "trips" of a kind for which India set the precedent for centuries.

Most remarkably, the song doesn't sort out its social satire from its implicitly positive treatment of drugs. Bob Dylan often puns with roughly the same intention, as in "Rainy Day Woman #12 & 35," a simple but effective example:

> Well, they'll stone you when you're trying to be so good,
> They'll stone you just like they said they would.
> They'll stone you when you try to go home,
> Then they'll stone you when you're there all alone.
> But I would not feel so all alone:
> Everybody must get stoned.

In the Beatles' song, the very same phrases that belong to the platitudes of the "beautiful people" belong also, with favorable connotations, not to be erased by their later criticisms of it, to the drug scene. The question, "And have you travelled very far?" is answered by Lennon, the "beautiful" person, with what socially would be a comfortable cliche: "Far as the eye can see." But the phrase is really too outmoded for the jet age and thus sends us back to the original question and to the possibility that the "travel" can refer to a "trip" on LSD, the destination of which would indeed be "as far as the eye can see." Most of the lyrics operate in this double way, both as social satire and drug talk: "How often have you been there? / Often enough to know," or "What did you see when you were there? / Nothing that doesn't show" or "Some do it naturally" (presumably an acidhead by nature) to which the answer is "Happy to be that way." The song could pass simply as social satire, though to see that and that only is also to be the object of satire, of not knowing what implications are carried even by the language you make fun of for its imprecisions. The point, and it's one that I'll come back to, is that the argot of LSD isn't much different from the banalities of question and answer between a "beautiful" person and his bedazzled interviewer. The punning genius of the group is evident here perhaps more effectively than in Lennon's two books, *In His Own Write* and *A Spaniard in the Works*, with their affinities to Edward Lear.

The Beatles are primarily musicians and musical composers, however, and don't choose to get stuck even within their most intricate verbal contrivances. They escape often by reminding us and themselves

117

that they are singers and not pushers, performers and not propagandists. The moment occurs in "Baby You're a Rich Man," as it does in other songs, near the end, in the question "Now that you've found another key / What are you going to play?" Necessarily the question refers us to their music, while at the same time alluding to the promised results of drugs — a new "key" to personality, to a role as well as to the notes that one might "play." Similar uses of words that can allude both to the subject of the moment and to their constant subject, musical creation, occur in "All You Need Is Love" ("Nothing you can sing that can't be sung"), with implications we'll get to in a moment, and in the second song on the *Sgt. Pepper* album, "A Little Help from My Friends." Sung by Ringo the "help" refers most simply to affection when there is no one around to love and it also means pot supplied by a friend. However, at the beginning of the song it explicitly means the assistance the others will give Ringo with his singing, while the phrases "out of tune" and "out of key" suggest, in the broadest sense, that the number, like the whole occasion, is in the mode not of the Beatles but of Sgt. Pepper's Lonely Hearts Club Band: "What would you think if I sang out of tune,/ Would you stand up and walk out on me. / Lend me your ears and I'll sing you a song, / And I'll try not to sing out of key. / Oh, I get by with a little help from my friends, / Mmmm, going to try with a little help from my friends, . . . "

One of the Beatles' most appealing qualities is, again, their tendency more to self-parody than to parody of others. The two are of course very close for performers who empathize with all the characters in their songs and whose most conspicuous moments of self-parody occur when they're emulating someone whose musical style they'd like to master. At such moments their boyishness really does shine forth as a musical virtue: giving themselves almost wholly to an imitation of some performer they admire, their necessary exaggeration of his style makes fun of no one so much as themselves. It's a matter of trying on a style and then — as if embarrassed by their own riches, by a self-confident knowledge that no style, not even one of their own invention, is more than a temporary exercise of strength — of laughing themselves out of imitation. Listen to the extravagant rendering on *Beatles '65* of Chuck Berry in "Rock and Roll Music" or their many early emulations of Presley, whose importance to their development is everywhere apparent, or the mimicry of Western Music in "Rocky Raccoon," or, especially, in "Act Naturally," on one of their best abums *Yesterday and Today*, or the McCartney imitation of Little Richard singing "Long Tall Sally" on the *Beatles Second Album*. It's all cowboys and Indians by people who have a lot of other games they want to play and who know very well where home is and when to go there.

118

Parody and self-parody is frequent among the other groups in the form of persistent stylization, but its object is almost always some clichéd sentiment or situation. Parody from the Beatles tends usually, and increasingly, to be directed toward musical tradition and their own musical efforts. This is at least one reason why "All You Need Is Love," recorded on the reverse side of "Baby, You're a Rich Man," is one of their most revealing. Along with the *Sgt. Pepper* album, it indicates so sophisticated an awareness of their historical achievements in music as to have made it evident that they could not continue much longer without still further changes of direction. There was always a chance of their creating such diverse possibilities for themselves that they would need, for that reason alone, to break up. "All You Need Is Love" is decisive evidence that when the Beatles think together (or apart) about anything they think musically and that musical thinking dictates their response to other things: to "love," in this instance, to drugs and social manners in "Baby, You're a Rich Man" and throughout the *Sgt. Pepper* album.

I'm so far from treating the Beatles in literary or merely verbal terms that I question whether or not any of the *subjects* of their songs would in itself prove a sufficient sustenance for their musical invention. The subject is first called forth and then kindled by some musical idea. At this point in their career it was impossible, given their and George Martin's musical knowledge and sophistication, that the title " All You Need Is Love" should mean what it would mean coming from any other group, namely hippie or flower love. Expectations of complications are satisfied from the outset: the repetition, three times and in a languorous tone, of the phrase "love, love, love" might remind us of the song of the aging Chaplin in *Limelight*, a song in which he keeps repeating the word throughout with a pitiable and insistent rapidity. Musical subterfuge of lyric simplicity occurs again when the title line, "all you need is love," picks up a musical trailer out of the thirties ballroom. The historical frequency of the "need" for love is thus proposed by the music, and it is as if this proposition emboldens the lyrics: "Nothing you can do that can't be done," "nothing you can sing that can't be sung," "nothing you can know that can't be known," "nothing you can see that can't be shown — it's easy" — this is a sample of equally ambiguous assertions that constitute the verbal substance of the song, even while the word "love" is being stretched out in choral background. And like the ambiguous language of "Baby, You're a Rich Man," the phrasing here sounds comfortably familiar — if you had love you could do anything.

Except that isn't really what the lyrics imply. Rather, the suggestion is that doing, singing, knowing, seeing have in some sense already been done, or at least that we needn't be in any particular

119

sweat about them; they're accepted as already within the accustomed range of human possibility. What has not been demonstrated to anyone's satisfaction, what hasn't been tried, is "love." "Love" remains the great unfulfilled need. But this sentiment occurs to them only *because* of the music. The historical evidence that love is still needed is in endless musical compositions about it. Far from suggesting that "love" will solve everything, which would be the hippie reading of "all you need is love," the song allows most things to be solved without it. Such a nice bit of discrimination emerges, again, from the music before it gets into the lyrics. Interestingly enough, the lyrics were meant to be simple in deference to the largely non-English-speaking audience for whom the song was especially written and performed on the BBC world-wide TV production of "Our World." "Normally," the Beatles' song publisher Richard James later observed, "the Beatles like to write sophisticated material, but they were glad to have the opportunity to write something with a very basic appeal." So was Shakespeare at the Globe, and we know, as a result, how unsophisticated he turned out to be. Whatever simplicity the piece has is entirely in the initial repetitions of title line and of the word "love," a verbal simplicity at once modified by the music and then turned into complications that have escaped even most English-speaking listeners.

Lennon and McCartney's musical recognition that the "need" for love is historical and recurrent is communicated less in the lyrics than by instrumental and vocal allusions to earlier material. The historical allusiveness is at the outset smart-alecky — the song opens with the French National Anthem — passes through the Chaplin echo, if that's what it is, to various echoes of the blues and boogie-woogie, all of them in the mere shadings of background, until at the end the song itself seems to be swept up and dispersed within the musical history of which it is a part and of the electronics by which that history has been made available. The process begins by a recurrence of the "love, love, love" phrase, here repeated and doubled as on a stalled record. It then proceeds into a medley of sounds, fractured, mingled musical phrases drifting into a blur which, as Paul Bertram pointed out to me, is like the sounds of a radio at night fading and drifting among the signals of different stations. We can make out fragments of old love songs condemned to wander through the airways for all time: "Greensleeves," a burst of classical trumpet sound, a hit of the thirties called "In the Mood," a ghostly "love you, yeah, yeah, yeah" of "She Loves You" from the *Beatles Second Album* of 1964 and, in the context of "All You Need Is Love," a pathetic "all together now . . . everybody!" of the old community sing. Far from being in any way satiric, the song gathers into itself the musical expression of the "need" for love as it has accumulated through decades of popular music.

This historical feeling for music, including their own musical creations, explains, I think, something centrally important about the Beatles: their fascination with the invented aspects of everything around them. They respond with a participatory tenderness and joy to styles and artifacts, and it is what makes them so attractively responsive, for older as well as younger listeners, to the human and social landscape of contemporary England. It's as if they naturally see the world in the form of *son et lumiere*: as they say in a beautiful neighborhood song about Liverpool, "Penny Lane is in my ears and in my eyes." Not everyone their age is capable of seeing the odd wonder of a meter maid — after all, a meter maid's a meter maid; fewer still would be moved to a song of praise like "Lovely Rita" ("When it gets dark I tow your heart away"); and only a Beatle could be expected, when seeing her with a bag across her shoulder, to have the historically enlivened vision that "made her look a little like a military man."

Now of course English boys out of Liverpool can be expected, it says here, to be more intimate than are American boys from San Francisco with the residual social and cultural evidences from World War II and even from the First World War. In response to these and other traces of the past, however, the Beatles display an absolutely unique kind of involvement. It isn't simply that they have an instinctive nostalgia for period styles, as in "She's Leaving Home" or "When I'm Sixty-four," or that they absorb the past through the media of the popular arts, through music, cinema, theatrical conventions, bands like Sgt. Pepper's or music-hall performers. Everyone to some extent apprehends the world in the shapes given it by the popular arts and its media; we all see even the things that are new to us through a gridiron of style.

No, the Beatles have the distinction in their work both of knowing that this is how they see and feel things and of enjoying the knowledge. It could be said that they guess what Beckett and Borges know but without any loss of simple enthusiasm or innocent expectation, and without any patronization of those who do not know. In the loving phrases of "Penny Lane," "A pretty nurse is selling poppies from a tray / And tho' she feels as if she's in a play, / She is anyway."

It isn't surprising that drugs have been important to their music, that members of the group joined an effort in England for the legalization of marijuana, partly as a result of the conviction and sentencing on drug charges of two of the Rolling Stones, and that in response to questions, Lennon, McCartney, and Harrison let it be known that they'd taken LSD. At least four of the songs on the *Sgt. Pepper* album are concerned with taking a "trip" or "turning on":

"A Little Help from My Friends," "Lucy in the Sky with Diamonds," "Fixing a Hole," and "A Day in the Life," with a good
chance of a fifth in "Getting Better." Throughout the album, the
consciousness of the *dramatis personae* has already been created by
the media and by the popular arts. Drugs are proposed as a kind of
personal escape into the freedom of an invention that at least seems
to be all one's own.

While inventing the world out of the mind with drugs is more
physically risky than doing it by writing songs or films or by wearing
costumes, it isn't danger that the songs offer for consideration. And
in any case it's up to the Beatles, or anyone else to decide for themselves what they want for their minds and bodies. Instead, the songs
propose something oddly reasonable about drugs: that the vision of
the world while on a "trip" isn't necessarily wilder than a vision of
the world through which we travel under the influence of the arts
or the news media. Thus, the third song on the album, "Lucy in the
Sky with Diamonds," proposes that the listener can "picture" a
"trip" scene without taking such a "trip" himself. Here, as in "Baby
You're a Rich Man," the experience of a "trip" is wittily superim-
posed on the experience of ordinary travel: "Picture yourself on a
train in a station, / With plasticine porters with looking glass ties, /
Suddenly someone is there at the turnstile, / The girl with kaleidoscope eyes." Of course the images could come as easily from Edward
Lear as from the experience of drugs, and Lennon has claimed that
the title of the song is not an anagram for LSD but was taken from a
drawing his son did at school. Lennon knows to the point of hilarity
that one meaning denies the hidden presence of another only to all
strangers and the police.

Still his reticence is obviously a form of the truth. The Beatles
won't be reduced to drugs when they mean, intend, and enact so
much more. "Acid," Harrison told the Los Angeles *Free Press* a few
months after these songs came out, "is not the answer, definitely not
the answer. It's enabled people to see a little bit more, but when
you really get hip, you don't need it." Later, to Hunter Davies of the
London *Sunday Times*, McCartney announced that they'd given up
drugs. "It was an experience we went through and now it's over and
we don't need it any more. We think we're finding other ways of
getting there." In this effort they were apparently influenced by
Maharishi Mahesh Yogi, the Indian founder of the International
Meditation Society, though even on the way to their initiation in
Bangor, North Wales, Lennon wondered if the experience wasn't
simply going to be another version of what they already knew: "You
know, like some are EMI and some Decca, but it's really still records."

122

Without even willing it, we "picture" ourselves much of the time anyway, see ourselves and the world through a screen of exotic images usually invented by someone else. This is the suggestion throughout the *Sgt. Pepper* album, most obviously on the cover, with its clustered photographs of world-shaping "stars" of all kinds. In "A Day in the Life," the last song and a work of great power and historical grasp, the hapless man whose role is sung by Lennon wants to "turn on" himself and his lover — maybe us too — as a relief from the multiple controls exerted over life and the imagination by various and competing media. He is further confounded by the fact that these controls often impose themselves under the guise of entertainment. "Oh boy" — that sad little interjection of enthusiasm comes from Lennon's sweet, vulnerable voice into orchestral movements of intimidating, sometimes portentous momentum:

> I read the news today oh boy
> About a lucky man who made the grade
> And though the news was rather sad
> Well I just had to laugh
> I saw the photograph.
> He blew his mind out in a car
> He didn't notice that the lights had changed
> A crowd of people stood and stared
> They'd seen his face before
> Nobody was really sure
> If he was from the House of Lords.
> I saw a film today oh boy
> The English Army had just won the war
> A crowd of people turned away
> But I just had to look
> Having read the book.
> I'd love to turn you on . . . .

The news in the paper is "rather sad" — as is the pun on "making the grade," a reference both to a man's success and to a car's movement up the road to what will be a crash — but the photograph is funny, so how does one respond to the suicide; suicide is a violent repudiation of the self but it mightn't have happened if the man had followed the orders of the traffic lights; the victim isn't so much a man anyway as a face people have seen someplace in the news, in photographs or possibly even on film; and while a film of the English army winning the war is too dated for most people to look at, and maybe they don't believe in the victory anyway, the man in the song has to look at it (oh boy — a film) because he has read a book about it and therefore it does have some reality for him.* "Turning on" is at least a way of escaping submission to the media designed to turn on the mind from the outside — quite appropriately the song was banned on the BBC. Loving to turn "you" on, either a lover or you, the listener, is an effort to escape the horror of loneliness projected by the final images of the song:

> I read the news today oh boy
> Four thousand holes in Blackburn
> Lancashire
> And though the holes were rather small
> They had to count them all
> Now they know how many holes it takes
> To fill the Albert Hall.
> I'd love to turn you on.

The audience in Albert Hall — the same as the "lovely audience" in the first song whom the Beatles would like to "take home" with them? — are only so many holes: unfilled and therefore unfertile holes, holes of decomposition, gathered together but separate and therefore countable, inarticulately alone, the epitome of so many "assholes." Is this merely a bit of visionary ghoulishness, something seen on a "trip"? No, good citizens can find it, like everything else in the song, either in the *Daily Mail*, where Lennon saw the reference, or in the report somewhat earlier of how Scotland Yard probed for buried bodies on a moor by making holes in the earth with poles and then waiting for the stench of decomposing flesh.

Lennon and McCartney in their songs seem as vulnerable as the man in "A Day in the Life" to the sights and sounds by which different media shape and then reshape reality. But their response isn't

---

*Amusingly enough, commentary on the Beatles is already as bedeviled as is commentary on the classics of English poetry by constricting and mostly irrelevant research, and it works in both cases usually to the impoverishment of poetry. Thus we can learn from Hunter Davies's useful biography, *The Beatles*, that the "lucky man who made the grade" and died in a car was based on Tara Brown, a friend of the Beatles who died in a motor accident; that "the film" alluded to is "How I Won the War" in which Lennon had just finished acting; that while Lennon was writing the song he had the *Daily Mail* propped up in front of him and saw there a paragraph about the discovery of 4000 holes in Blackburn, Lancashire. But the song's characterization of the man and the circumstances of his death make any knowledge of Mr. Brown merely obstructive; the Lennon in the film obviously is only possibly the Lennon of the song who says he just had to look at the film because he'd "read the book"; and the 4000 holes are given so many meanings in the song as altogether to release speculation from fact. — R.P.

in any way as intimidated, and "turning on" isn't their only recourse. They can also tune in, literally to show how one shaped view of reality can be mocked out of existence by crossing it with another. They mix their media the way they mix musical sounds; lyrics in one tone are crossed with music in quite another; and they do so with a vengeance. It's unwise ever to assume that they're doing only one thing musically or expressing themselves in only one style. "She's Leaving Home" does have a persistent cello background to evoke genteel melodrama of an earlier decade, and "When I'm Sixty-four" is intentionally clichéd throughout both in its ragtime rhythm and in its lyrics. The result is a satiric heightening of the love-nest sentimentality of old popular songs in the mode of "He'll build a little home / Just meant for two / From which I'll never roam / Who would, would you?" The home in "When I'm Sixty-four" is slightly larger to accommodate children, but that's the only important difference: "Every summer we can rent a cottage / In the Isle of Wight, if it's not too dear / We shall scrimp and save / Grandchildren on your knee / Vera, Chuck, & Dave." But the Beatles aren't satisfied merely with having written a brilliant spoof, with scoring, on their own authority, off of death-dealing clichés. Instead, they quite suddenly at the end transform one cliché (of sentimental domesticity) into another (of a lonely-hearts newspaper advertisement), thereby proposing a vulgar contemporary medium suitable to the cheap and public sentiments that once passed for nice, private, and decent: "Send me a postcard, drop me a line, / Stating point of view / Indicate precisely what you mean to say / Yours sincerely, wasting away / Give me your answer, fill in a form / Mine for evermore / Will you still need me, will you still feed me. / When I'm sixty-four."

The *Sgt. Pepper* album and the singles released just before and after it — "Penny Lane," "Strawberry Fields Forever," "All You Need Is Love," and "Baby, You're a Rich Man" — constituted the Beatles' most audacious musical effort up to that point, works of such achieved ambitiousness as to give an entirely new retrospective shape to their whole career. Nothing less is being claimed by these songs than that the Beatles exist not merely as a phenomenon of entertainment but as a force of historical consequence. They have placed themselves within a musical, and historical environment more monumental in its surroundings and more significantly populated than was the environment of any of their earlier songs. Listening to the *Sgt. Pepper* album one thinks not simply of the history of popular music but of the history of this century. It doesn't matter that some of the songs were composed before it occurred to the Beatles to use the motif of Sgt. Pepper, with its historical overtones; the songs emanated from some inwardly felt coherence that awaited a merely explicit design, and they would ask to be heard together even without design.

Under the aegis of an old-time concert given by the type of music-hall band with which Lennon's father, Alfred, claims to have been associated, the songs offer something like a review of contemporary English life. They are saved from folksong generality, however, by having each song resemble a dramatic monologue. The review begins with the *Sgt. Pepper* theme song, followed immediately by "A Little Help from My Friends": Ringo, helped by the other Beatles, will, as I've already mentioned, try not to sing out of "key." He will try, that is, to fit into a style still heard in England though very much out of date. Between this and the reprise of *Sgt. Pepper*, which would be the natural end of the album, are ten songs, and while some are period pieces, about hangovers from the past, as is the band itself, no effort is made at any sort of historical chronology. Their arrangement is apparently haphazard, suggesting how the hippie and the historically pretentious, the genteel and the mod, the impoverished and the exotic, the India influence and the influence of technology, are inextricably entangled into what is England. As I probably shouldn't say again, the Beatles never for long wholly submerge themselves in any form or style. Thus, at the end of the Indian, meditative sonorities of "Within You, Without You" the burst of laughter can be taken to mean — look, we really have come through. It's an assurance from the Beatles (if it is in fact their laughter and not the response of technicians left in the recording as an example of how "straights" might react to it) that they are still the Beatles, Liverpool boys still themselves on the far side of a demanding foreign experience.

So characteristic a release of themselves from history and back to their own proper time and place occurs with respect to the design of the whole album in a most poignant way. Right after the reprise of the Sgt. Pepper song, with no interval and picking up the beat of the Sgt. Pepper theme, an "extra" song, perhaps the most brilliant ever written by Lennon and McCartney, breaks out of the theatrical frame and transports us to "a day in the life," to the way we live now. Indeed, the degree of loneliness it projects could not be accommodated within the conventions of Sgt. Pepper's Lonely Hearts Club Band. Released from the controls of Sgt. Pepper, the song exposes the horrors of more contemporary and less benign controls. And it is from these that the song proposes the necessity of still further release. It does so in musical sounds meant to convey a "trip" out, sounds of ascending-airplane velocity and crescendo that occur right after the first "I'd love to turn you on," at midpoint in the song, and again after the final plaintive repetition of the line at the end, when the airplane sounds give way to a sustained orchestral chord

126

that drifts softly and slowly toward the induced illusion of infinity and silence. It is, as I've suggested, a song of wasteland, and the concluding "I'd love to turn you on" has as much propriety to the fragmented life that precedes it in the song and in the whole work as does the "Shantih, Shantih, Shantih" to the fragments of Eliot's poem. Eliot can be remembered here for still other reasons: not only because he pays conspicuous respect to the music hall but because his poems, like the Beatles' songs, work for a kaleidoscopic effect, for fragmented patterns of sound that can bring historic masses into juxtaposition only to let them be fractured by other emerging and equally evocative fragments.

Eliot is not among the sixty-two faces and figures, all unnamed and in some cases quite obscure, gathered round the Beatles on the cover. Pictorially this extends the collage effect so significant to the music. In making the selection, the Beatles were drawn, as one might expect, to figures who promote the idea of other possible worlds or who offer literary and cinematic trips to exotic places: Poe, Oscar Wilde, H.G. Wells, along with Marx, Jung, Lawrence of Arabia and Johnny Weissmuller. Understandably, the Beatles are also partial to the kind of theatrical person whose full being seems equivalent to the theatrical self, like W.C. Fields, Tom Mix, Marlon Brando, and Mae West, who has delightfully managed to adapt the Beatle's "Day Tripper" to her own style.

Above all, the cover is a celebration of the Beatles themselves, who can now be placed (and Bob Dylan, too) within that tiny group who have, aside from everything else they've done, infused the imagination of the living with the possibilities of other ways of living, of extraordinary existences, of something beyond "a day in the life." The record was a bit like a funeral for the Beatles, except that they'd be no more "dead" than anyone else in attendance.There they are in the center, mustachioed and in the brassed and tasseled silk of the old-time bands, and with brilliant, quite funny implications, they are also represented in the collage as wax figures by Madame Tussaud, clothed in business suits. Live Beatles in costumes from the past and effigies of the Beatles in the garb of the present, with the name Beatles in flowers planted before the whole group — this bit of slyness is of a piece with not sorting out past and present and promised future in the order of the songs, or in the mixed allusiveness to period styles, including earlier Beatles' styles, or in the confoundings of media in songs like "When I'm Sixty-four" or "A Day in the Life." The cover suggests that the Beatles to some extent live the past in the present, live in the shadows of their own as well as of other people's past performances, and that among the imaginative creations that fascinate them most, the figures closest at hand on

127

the cover, are their own past selves. "And the time will come," it is promised in one of their songs, when you will see we're all one, and life flows on within you and without you." As an apprehension of artistic, and perhaps of any other kind of placement within living endeavor, this classical idea is allowable only to the most generous spirits and the greatest performers.

Introduction to
THE BEATLES IN PERSPECTIVE

Not everyone was as impressed as Messrs. Chasins, Holroyd and Poirier. "The Beatles in Perspective," by John Gabree, appeared in *Down Beat* in late 1967 as a reaction to the acclaim that the group received in the wake of **Sergeant Pepper**. The Beatles had been given too much credit as the leading innovators of pop music, according to Gabree. Although enormously popular, they were hardly the "messengers from beyond rock and roll," as they were hailed from the pages of *Time* ("The Messengers," September 22, 1967, pages 60--68).

Gabree's piece drew fire on the pages of *Down Beat* itself. In "I'm Looking Through You" (*Down Beat*, January 11, 1968, pages 18–19), Pete Welding defends the Beatles, accusing Gabree of "convenient omissions, distortions, or fanciful interpretations of fact."

"The Beatles in Perspective" later became the basis for the first chapter of Gabree's *The World of Rock* (Fawcett Publications, 1968).

THE BEATLES IN PERSPECTIVE

by John Gabree

It is important to get this straight: the Beatles never have been in the vanguard of pop music. They are not now and are unlikely ever to be.

The group's impact has been staggering, but it has been mostly sociological and only negligibly musical. Beatlephiles admit that the early work of the masters was largely imitative ("revitalizing," "opened our eyes to what was right in our own back yards," etc.). But, they argue, the Beatles then went on to become the avant garde, the pacesetters of pop music. This is quite simply not true.

There is a good and obvious reason why and how this confusion developed: most critics don't know their rock. Most people who write about rock today probably weren't listening a year ago, certainly not two, and aren't really listening now. They come in late, already thinking the Beatles are it. They pick up *Revolver* or *Sgt. Pepper* and have a revelation. But very few are willing to take the foursome's work for what it is: an introduction to a world of creative adventure, of which the Beatles are merely the popularizers, not the creators.

My first reaction to the recent *Time* cover story on the Beatles was to go blank (which is quite often my reaction to *Time* cover stories). *Time*'s reporter, Luce-ly flinging about half (in)formed judgments about pop music, turned in an essay full of deft cracks about "the rhythmic caterwauling of Elvis Presley" and the "doldrum of derivative mewing by white singers," etc., none of it much to the point.

Later I realized that though the *Time* article *is* wrong-headed, it is, sadly, no more so than most writing on rock. The only critic with any perspective on the Beatles, for example, is Richard Goldstein of the *Village Voice*. The New York *Times*, not surprisingly, has introduced a chap named Tom Phillips, whose entire raison d'etre seems to be to defend the Beatles from Goldstein. To the popular press, the Beatles are the darlings of the day, the Andy Warhols of rock.

131

The real story is this:

In the late '50s, white rock, like the rest of pop culture, was at a low. Things weren't quite as bad as Beatle-lovers like to pretend, but they weren't good. There was a doldrum, all right, produced by the ennui excreted in such massive doses during the Eisenhower years. With Kennedy came change. After 1960, the civil rights movement caught fire, and black culture became a focus of attention. Simultaneously, activist youth turned to folk music, looking for an outlet with more meaning than could be derived from Bobby Rydell and his friends from Philadelphia.

Presley and the Everly Brothers, meanwhile, had been away in the Army (and anyway, Presley had sold his soul to Hal Wallis), Jerry Lee Lewis and Chuck Berry had been driven off for performing unmentionable nasties, Buddy Holly was dead, and Fats Domino and Little Richard in retirement, leaving poor Chubby Checker, a sort of musical Uncle Tom, alone on the stage. Everybody else was black, which the communications media viewed like death and still do.

Perhaps it was inevitable that the revitalization of pop music would occur through a medium, the Beatles, that filtered out the elements that mass cultists found offensive — you can only get to C from A by going to B, but, if B was a necessary intermediate step, it should not have been allowed to become a hangup. In physics experiments, a balloon that would be small under normal circumstances inflates out of proportion when introduced into a pressureless glass bell. That is what happened to the Beatle balloon when it was inserted into the vacuum of pop music in the early '60s.

I first heard the Beatles while standing in front of the record store on the corner of Thayer and Angell streets in Providence, R.I. A raucous imitation of the Isley Brothers' *Twist and Shout* was blaring from a speaker inside. Like much of their work since then, the cut was a mediocre copy, but unlike most of their duplications it reached a smaller audience than the original.

Their brashness made it immediately evident that the Beatles *had* to catch on. They were fresh, while American pop music hadn't produced a new face of lasting significance in a half-dozen years. They had a good ear for harmony and a nearly perfect sense of taste when choosing whom to imitate. They sounded raw and vital when compared with their vapid contemporaries on the Top 40 stations. But they were also safe, being white and having none of that aggressive sexuality that had been so upsetting in the likes of Elvis — all they wanted to do, remember, was hold your hand.

Their playing and singing during this early period was thoroughly unimaginative, not to say monotonous, and what we seek today, if we listen at all to songs like *I Want to Hold You Hand* or *She Loves*

132

You (the latter unaccountably called *Yeah, Yeah, Yeah* by the percipient Phillips), is nostalgia rather than musical pleasure.

With that sure sense of self-preservation that always had characterized the Establishment, America embraced the Beatles. At a time when the civil rights movement was at an all-time high of enthusiasm and seeming success, when we were becoming involved in an unpopular war in Southeast Asia, when much of the cream of our youth was opting for non-Establishment solutions to anti-Establishment goals, when rhythm-and-blues and country-and-western abounded with authentic talent, when the folk music revolution had already produced Bob Dylan and a revived interest in the blues — in the midst of all this we settled for very thin soup in rock-and-roll.

Jazz, which has not been widely accepted in pop circles since the end of the big war, offers no parallel situation (except, perhaps, the West Coast jazz phenomenon), but folk music provides an interesting example of a group that performed the same function as the Beatles now do for rock. The Weavers were a highly eclectic (the word is used more than any other in connection with the Beatles) folk quartet that was central in attracting the pop cultists and intellectuals to folk music in the '50s. Without the Weavers, there could have been no folk revolution at the beginning of this decade. In the same way, it is hoped, the pop critics and, more important, the audiences who have recently discovered the Beatles, will be tempted to look beyond them to see what is really happening.

Probably the change will come, but so far it hasn't. For now the press, the pop-cultists, the Establishment, are using the Beatles to make it possible to ignore more significant happenings, happenings that are genuine responses to the fact that this society is in trouble, and happenings they cannot tolerate. There is, for example, an increasing alienation (which even poor *Time* is aware of) that is making itself felt in a variety of ways: the nonviolent peace movement has failed, and the black community seems increasingly taken with the angry rhetoric of black power; the horrible, pointless, corrosive war in Vietnam has finally undermined our blind faith in the government, seriously impaired whatever value there was in the President's domestic program, inspired rejection of U.S. involvement in the affairs of other nations, and drowned the spirits and hopes of many. Cities are in flames, while Congress fiddles; the black and the poor are demonstrating a new-found militancy; materialism, greed, and lack of concern for others seem to characterize the national posture; and the young are forever reminded of their essential powerlessness.

The reaction of youth to all this has been threefold: activist alienation of the black power, ghetto-organizing, rent-strike, draft-resistance variety on the left, and sour yearnings for the 18th century on the right; hippie alienation of the turn-on, tune-in, drop-out type;

or simple alienation of the good old silent '50s style. Not a very happy collection of alternatives.

It is not unfair to the Beatles to say that they are relevant to none of this. Their job — and they have done it well — has been to travel a few miles behind the avant garde, consolidating gains and popularizing new ideas.

The criticism for their undeserved domination of the scene must be directed at the press and the media who have deified the Beatles at the cost of neglecting more adventuresome creators in rock. (On a recent morning, a Chicago disc jockey, who gets a lot of mileage out of some supposed connection with the Beatles — and who somewhat tastelessly played *A Day in the Life* in honor of Brian Epstein before it finally was decided he had not killed himself — spun, at a listener's request, *I'm So Glad* by Cream, one of the best of the experimental groups, and then spent several moments savagely and unnecessarily putting the group down.) Kept in perspective, the Beatles are obviously a vitally important group, as for that matter are the Monkees and Herman's Hermits, but it's useless to contend that musically they are movers and makers.

None of this is a comment on the Beatles as individuals, or as pop leaders in nonmusical ways. When John Lennon responded to an interviewer's stock question about the origin of the group's name with the story of a figure that one day rose out of the sea, pointed at them, and said, "You're Beatles — with an *a*," he provided an example of healthy looseness and irreverence that has had a strong influence on the new left-style of the young. And certainly their support of marijuana reform legislation and their admission to having used LSD are courageous acts. And if everything that has been said in advance about *How I Won the War* is true, Lennon has taken a significant stand against war.

On the other hand, they have been at the escapist end of the range of artistic responses possible to the phenomena of the '60s: not apolitical in the manner of the Lovin' Spoonful or Herman's Hermits, they are political in that clouded way usually associated with liberal U.S. politics. Their movies, *Help* and *A Hard Day's Night*, can be viewed as dramatizations of the whole male-adventure-fantasy syndrome, and they succumbed quite completely to manager Epstein's attempt to make them camp heroes, as wholesome as bread pudding.

What they have accomplished, besides demonstrating excellent taste in their selection of influences, is to write several first-rate compositions. especially the compassionate *Eleanor Rigby*, and produce two or three pop masterpieces (*Eleanor Rigby* and *A Day in the Life*) and one brilliant album, *Revolver*. The album was important because, with the Rolling Stones' *Aftermath* (released about the same time), it constituted a summation of previous developments in rock.

Here were the blues, hard-rock, ballads, Near Eastern and jazz harmonics, c&w, baroque, etc. In addition, *Revolver*, like *Aftermath*, was restrained and dignified, eschewing the sensationalism that must have been a tremendous temptation for both groups, and which the Beatles have finally given in to in *Sgt. Pepper's Lonely Hearts Club Band*. With rare exceptions, none of the compositions in the latter album have the melodic quality so often present previously in their work. Gone, too, is the restraint, the tastefulness that used to signal them when to stop. The affectation of "unity" is a sham – and a seeming afterthought – that has been seized on by the reviewers. The press got so silly that even the *Christian Science Monitor* hailed the album's release with a gushy editorial (as still more trail blazing by the fantastic Beatles), managing at the same time never to mention that the Who are performing rock mini-operas or that there is a rock oratorio on each side of the Mothers of Invention's *Absolutely Free*.

There are only two reasons why *Sgt. Pepper* deserves to be more modestly acclaimed. *A Day in the Life* is a harshly ironic performance juxtaposing Lennon's introverted ramblings (*I read the news today, oh boy/About a lucky man who made the grade*) against McCartney's flat recounting of the day's events (*Found my coat and grabbed my hat/Made the bus in seconds flat*). And the album as a whole reinforces the importance of electronics in future pop and rock.

But these are not techniques that originated with the Beatles, and they are not even used by them in terribly original ways. There already had been excellent studio work on albums and singles by the Byrds, Donovan, the Beach Boys, and others, including Judy Collins' brilliantly eclectic *In My Life*. The question here also becomes whether we are to credit the group, the producer, or the engineer. I have heard – and whether it is apocryphal or true, it is true enough – that *A Day in the Life* was born when the Beatles' producer, engineer, and musical midwife, George Martin, soldered together the strands of two separate compositions. Shouldn't we laud Martin instead of the quartet?

More important, however, is the fact that *Sgt. Pepper*, only a slight technical improvement on *Revolver*, has already been left behind by the work of other groups: The "operettas" of the Mothers of Invention; Who's dynamic performances and advanced compositions; the Yardbirds' newfound assurance; Cream's brilliant experimentation; the advanced blues stylings of Canned Heat and Big Brother and the Holding Co.; the unique and adventuresome psychedelic experiments of Jefferson Airplane, Grateful Dead, and Country

Joe and the Fish; jazz-rock explorations by the Gary Burton-Larry Coryell team and by Jeremy Steig and the Satyrs; and the continuing excellence of the Rolling Stones.

The Stones present the most telling case. They started in about the same place as the Beatles, with perhaps a shade more expertise, a brilliant vocalist in Mick Jagger, and an orientation that leaned closer to a purely blues-based style. Jagger and Keith Richard developed quickly into songwriters comparable to Lennon and McCartney, and anyone else you might choose to name. But they have been ignored by the press — except for an occasional finger of admonishment — mostly because they provide a musical parallel to the civil rights movement, the anti-Vietnam war protests, and the sexual and drug revolutions. They are almost the very embodiments of the alienation the pop cultists would like to ignore.

John Goodman, writing in the *New Leader*, points out that "as to themes, the Stones like to satirize sex, the everyday, drugs, and the cool attitude. In the album *Flowers*, the red-eyed chick on drugs is put down hard: 'You may look pretty, but I can't say the same for your mind' (*Ride on, Baby*). *Mother's Little Helper*, the yellow pill 'helps her on her way, gets through her busy day,' with ironic consequences. In *Between the Buttons* yesterday's girls are like *Yesterday's Papers* — who wants them? But the Stones' finest scorn is reserved for those women of affectation who are *Complicated* or *Cool, Calm, and Collected*. The humor here is winning, for it is both bitter and warm, reflective and spontaneous. The Stones have learned how to make their protest mature, viable, and musical."

The only point left to emphasize is that they are authentic originals who have been content to go their own way, sometimes in the face of considerable opposition. For example, few groups would have had the chutzpah to release *Let's Spend the Night Together*; in Beatledom, this would never happen.

In reaction to the emphasis in the hippie community on love in its various manifestations, the Beatles felt compelled to honor the subject in song. Not sure which way the wind was blowing and not wanting to be left either pro- or anti-love, they compromised with a mindless composition called *All You Need Is Love*. The result of their confusion is a mishmash that delights writer Phillips as much as it confuses him. The Stones, meanwhile, produced *We Love You*, a much more assured and inventive song, which managed to be warmly ironic about love and to satirize the Beatles at the same time. The argument is not that art must serve politics, or even that an artist must deal with political issues, but it is necessary to point out that the songs and performances of the Beatles have all been executed with clearly prescribed limitations imposed by the desires and needs of the disseminators of pop, the radio and television outlets, the press, and lately the intellectual and "concerned" magazines.

It has been suggested to me by one correspondent that the Beatles are really a contemporary equivalent of Hector Berlioz, a composer whose unengaged romanticism expressed itself in brilliantly orchestrated productions of quite ordinary musical ideas. In the same way, the Beatles never achieve the tension that underlies all great art. Nor have they, except on rare occasions, written memorable compositions. Lovely often but memorable seldom. Art must simply be true to itself, and this I believe, is the Beatles' failure. The foursome has been compared to Johnny Appleseed, sowing musical seeds, but they have really spent the last four years picking apples in other peoples' orchards to make their own (sometimes delicious) pies.

As *Time* approvingly points out, throughout their career the Beatles have maintained "their exemplary behavior." Who can help but embrace four such charming lads who can have the good sense to proclaim — as they do stolidly on *Sgt. Pepper* — in the disintegrating fall of 1967, "I have to admit it's getting better — it's getting better all the time?"

DISCOGRAPHY

Beatles, MGM 4215
Meet the Beatles, Capitol 2047
Beatles' Second Album, Capitol 2080
Hard Day's Night, Beatles, United Artists 3366, 6366
Beatles '65, Capitol 2228
Something New, Beatles, Capitol 2108
Beatles' Story, Capitol TBO-2222
The Early Beatles, Capitol 2309
Beatles VI, Capitol 2358
Help!, Beatles, Capitol MAS-2386
Rubber Soul, Beatles, Capitol 2442
This Is Where It Started, Beatles, Metro 563
Yesterday & Today, Beatles, Capitol 2553
Revolver, Beatles, Capitol 2576
Sgt. Pepper's Lonely Hearts Club Band, Beatles, Capitol MAS-2653
Very Best of the Everly Brothers, Warner Bros. 1554
Twist and Shout, Isley Brothers, Wand 653
Buddy Holly's Greatest Hits, Coral 57492
Little Richard's Greatest Hits, Okeh 12121, 14121
Blue Suede, Elvis Presley, RCA Victor LPM/LSP-1254
Chuck Berry's Greatest Hits, Chess 1485
The Blues, Vol. 1--5, Cadet
Aftermath, Rolling Stones, London 3476, 476

Between the Buttons, Rolling Stones, London 3499, 499
Flowers, Rolling Stones, London 3509, 509
Byrds' Greatest Hits, Columbia CL-2716, CS-9516
Real, Donovan, Hickory 135
Mellow Yellow, Donovan, Epic LN-24239, BN-26239
Pet Sounds, Beach Boys, Capitol 2458
In My Life, Judy Collins, Elektra 320
Bringing It Back Home, Bob Dylan, Columbia CL-2328, CS-9128
Highway 61 Revisited, Bob Dylan, Columbia CL-2389, CS-9189
Blonde on Blonde, Bob Dylan, Columbia C2L-41, C2S-841
Bob Dylan's Greatest Hits, Columbia KCL-2663, KCS-9463
Mothers of Invention, Verve 5005
Absolutely Free, Mothers of Invention, Verve 5013
Yardbirds, Epic LN-24167, BN-26167
Yardbirds' Greatest Hits, Epic LN-24246, BN-26246
Having a Rave Up, Yardbirds, Epic LN-24177, BN-26177
Little Games, Yardbirds, Epic LN-24313, BN-26313
OverUnderSideways, Yardbirds, Epic LN-24210, BN-26210
Yardbirds with Sonny Boy Williamson, Mercury 21071, 61071
My Generation, Who, Decca 4664
Happy Jack, Who, Decca 4892
Fresh Cream, Cream, Atco 33-206
Canned Heat, Liberty LRP-3526, LST-7526
Big Brother and the Holding Company, Mainstream 56099, S-6099
Grateful Dead, Warner Bros. 1689
Jefferson Airplane, RCA Victor LPM/LSP-3584
Surrealistic Pillow, Jefferson Airplane, LPM/LSP-3766
Country Joe and the Fish, Vanguard 9244
Tennessee Firebird, Gary Burton, RCA Victor LPM/LSP 3719
Duster, Gary Burton, RCA Victor LPM/LSP-3835
Blaze, Herman's Hermits, MGM 4478
Best of the Lovin' Spoonful, Kama 8056

Introduction to
ICONIC MODES: THE BEATLES

Frank Sinatra, Elvis Presley and the Beatles were all teen idols. Young fans worshipped them. In "Iconic Modes: The Beatles," a discussion of the Group as an icon of culture, Ralph Brauer suggests a literal interpretation of the "idol" part of the phrase "teen idol."

ICONIC MODES: THE BEATLES

by Ralph Brauer

"Yeah, well, if there is a God, we're all it."
John Lennon

"God," noted Pogo from his vantage point in the comics, "is unemployed." Words have been discarded, retooled, or vulgarized accordingly. "Idol" now pertains to anyone or anything to the group doing the idolizing. For example, a high school sports hero can be an idol to a grade school sandlot jock while his older sisters "just idolize Paul Newman's eyes." Charisma is no longer a word applied only to religious figures who have received a special grace from God; instead a political hero like John Kennedy can be said to have "that special grace" and a TV newscaster like Walter Cronkite is spoken of as having charisma. Icon has come to be a word used by cultural analysis to describe images which in Marshall Fishwick's words "are admired artifacts, external expressions of internal convictions, everyday things that make everyday meaningful."[1]

It is a pointed comment on our world today that some like Fishwick believe icons can only be objects. Although the religious figures of the medieval icons were materially dead, they were still spiritually alive and their presence was felt as surely by their devotees as if they had been living. Death and life did not have the same meaning then as they do now. To see our contemporary icons as being only objects is to too literally interpret the medieval icon and in turn cut off from our understanding the study of the cultural significance of people who have affected our experience in iconographic ways. To say for instance that a poster of James Dean is an icon, that perhaps his role in *Rebel Without a Cause* could be, but that the living individual could not is to draw an all too literal line between life and death, person and object, thing and no thing, which circumscribes rather than enlarges our understanding. If we are to use the concept of icons to gain an understanding of the deep visions and values of our culture we must examine those individuals as well as those objects which we endow with our beliefs in their sacredness. As Fishwick

141

put it, "what is central to the concept of icon is touching a center near man's essence."[2]

In contemporary America perhaps nothing touches the center of certain people as much as our popular music stars. American teenagers, especially girls, place on their walls pictures or posters of their favorite pop idols and surround them with other objects of devotion — concert tickets, record jackets, and perhaps, if they are lucky enough and impertinent enough, a lock of hair, a cufflink, a ripped piece of clothing. Like pieces of the True Cross or vials of the Holy Blood, these objects from the person of the pop star are deeply venerated. They may well be kept in specially designed reliquaries. Unlike their religious counterparts, though, these pop icons are only temporal. Their devotees grow up or find new objects of veneration. Even the most devoted admirer of Donny Osmond ultimately knows that some day the picture, tickets and other objects will end up in the trash can.

During most of the sixties there were probably no pop stars as high on the iconography scale as the Beatles. Their devotees came from every class and age group. Many of them willingly had their hair clipped in imitation of their idols (whose haircuts resembled those worn by monks in many a Hollywood movie — perhaps that's why their imitators were called Monkees) or invested five to ten bucks in a similarly styled wig. Others bought collarless jackets and a type of leather boot which came to be called, appropriately enough, "Beatle boots." Original posters from their concerts sold in galleries for astronomical prices. Yellow submarines appeared on the sides of brick buildings. Thousands of children were named after them as were stores, free schools, amusement parks and a host of products. Above all, though, we bought their records — and in greater volume than we have ever bought records from a single group or individual. We made millionaires of four plain lads from Liverpool along with a multitude of managers, merchandizers and assorted hangers-on and rip-off artists. We made those records so popular that today they are still used to draw in customers when sold at a discount. Revivals on radio are so frequent one wonders whether they ever really "left" us.

Like true devotees we spent hours discussing and memorizing the verses of these recorded "texts." Decyphering them became a world-wide pastime. Even the photographs on the album covers were analyzed. When rumor spread that cypher experts had determined that certain messages spoke of Paul's death, even the real Paul had trouble denying it.

Then there were the rites at which the Beatles themselves presided: those live concerts where all one could hear were literally thousands of screaming, shrieking, hysterical people. Only at brief moments could you catch slices of the music, but since you had heard it before, your mind filled in the blank spots. What was important above all else at these rites was to show your devotion, to show how *they* moved you, how much you felt about *them*, what it did to you. Ushers spoke in awe of the wet seats left by teenage girls. As John Lennon tells it in *Lennon Remembers* many of these female devotees went a great deal further in satisfying their sexual stirrings. According to Lennon the Beatles on tour resembled something from Fellini's *Satyricon*: "We had four bedrooms separate from . . . tried to keep them out of our room. And Derek's and Neil's rooms were always full of fuck knows what."[3]

For all Lennon's efforts to set the record straight, though, most of the Beatles' fan preferred to keep their sexual stirrings in the realm of fantasy. This fantasizing about the private lives of pop icons, of course, has a long history. Its most prominent exponents have always been the gossip columnists and the Hollywood fanzines. For rock fans the biggest fanzine of all was and still is *Rolling Stone*, which comes in tabloid form like the *National Enquirer* and at its best is an articulate alternative to the regular press, while at its worst it is nothing but a gossip sheet and trend spotter.

It was in *Rolling Stone* that Lennon finally, as he put it in the language of these times, "let it all hang out." In his remarks about the Beatles one senses a strong self-destructive tendency — about which I'll say more later — which in its attempt at realism rings not unlike the criticisms of the Beatles that were issued throughout their reign as pop icons.

No icon is without its iconoclasts — you cannot have one without the other. They are the negative image of the icon and their attacks on the icon help to define it, many times help to fuel its power, and probably tell us as much about the icon as those who are its devotees. During the sixties these iconoclasts (who would, no doubt, become quite heated at being so labelled) were by and large represented by what was then known as the Establishment. These Establishment/iconoclasts decried the early Beatles in unison, viewing them as shallow popular artists bent on making money or as long-haired corrupters of youth. Then as the Beatles' music grew more complex, the Establishment splintered. Liberal intellectuals suddenly began embracing the Beatles, proclaiming their profundity in such journals as *The Partisan Review*. College campuses were full of professors lecturing about the musical and cultural significance of the latest Beatles album. Looking back on it one can see that this splintering of the Establishment presaged the deeper split which was to break out openly in 1968. Suddenly the Blue Meanies became real — Blue Meanies being the name given the Chicago cops by protestors at the Democratic Convention.

143

The Blue Meanies becoming real marked the beginning of the end for the Beatles. In the heated conflicts of the late sixties and early seventies their music became middle-of-the-road. The *White Album* is a good example of the Beatles' inability to cope with the new times. It never presents a consistent unified whole as *Pepper* did. Jann Wenner reviewing the album at the time prophetically remarked that the album seemed the work of four individuals rather than a group. So like the rest of us in those time, the Beatles fragmented.

Ironically it was the love of the intellectuals which helped to kill the Beatles. Even though they were embraced by only part of the Establishment, that embrace was a slow strangle-hold which eventually would kill them. Hearing their professors lecture about the Beatles, the students, who had been the largest group of devotees of the pop idols, began to wonder about the quartet. This is because there is perhaps no surer kiss of death in the pop music business than for a performer to be embraced by the Establishment — to be analyzed, lectured on and written about. I can remember my own sickness on seeing Poirier's article "Learning from the Beatles" — if the Beatles could be learned from like a book, if professors could write papers about them, then their music had no power.

In pop music above all, power, especially a power that had the magic of the Beatles, was not something that could or should be discussed logically. Like the devotees of medieval religious icons, devotees of contemporary pop icons relate to the power and the magic of their idols. The ultimate paradox of the pop idol is that in this business of packaging and selling music as if it were a car or deodorant, the pop idol must have that indefinable something that cannot be lectured about.

There must be what Erich Neumann in *Art and the Creative Unconscious* called a numinous quality in the pop icon. Neumann speaks of this quality throughout his book as being that transcendent, other-worldly element that all great art and artists possess.

> The need of his times works inside the artist without his wanting it, seeing it, or understanding its true significance. In this sense he is closer to the seer, the prophet, the mystic. And it is precisely when he does not represent the existing canon but transforms and overturns it that his function rises to the level of the sacral, for he then gives utterance to the authentic and direct revelation of the numinosum.[4]

Neumann borrowed the term numinous from the theologian Rudolf Otto who coined it to describe the essence of the religious experience. Otto's book, *The Idea of the Holy* is a lengthy attempt to outline the elements of the numinous experience, yet from the beginning he knew he was trying to articulate the inarticulate. It

144

was for him an attempt to describe a deep emotional and intellectual experience which went beyond our individual consciousnesses.[5]

This numinous quality which Neumann found in great art and Otto found in religion, Franz Neumann found in the charismatic leader.[6] The quality possessed by the pop icons is certainly quite similar to that possessed by charismatic religious and political — leader figures as opposite and yet the same as Christ and Hitler — and by Erich Neumann's great artist figure of Leonardo Da Vinci.

That pop icons possess this numinous quality can be seen in looking at a figure like James Dean. As David Dalton describes Dean in his book *James Dean: The Mutant King*, Dean "like Gatsby . . . 'sprang from his Platonic conception of himself' and in this form carried his incorruptible dream through the movies and into our lives, . . . What happened to Jimmy became a record of what was happening to America."[7] Dean was a mutant and "the mutant must arise to make transition from the old organism to the new, . . . Mutant derives its meaning from the same root as myth and James Dean became a myth through his mutations, a mystery we will never completely comprehend."[8]

It is interesting that Dean — a pop idol — should possess qualities that have been associated with charismatic leaders because Max Weber's original use of charisma — and Weber was the one who gave the term its contemporary context — was to describe leaders whose power went beyond bureaucratic structures in an irrational way. As Weber saw him the charismatic leader was one who was opposed to the rational rules and normal routines of a bureaucratic society. "In contrast to any kind of bureaucratic organization of offices the charismatic structure knows nothing of a form or of an ordered procedure of appointment or dismissal . . . . The charismatic leader gains and maintains authority solely by proving his strength in life."[9]

Like Weber's political charismatic leader who functions against and beyond bureaucratic society, so our popular icons function against and beyond popular norms. Like James Dean, the Beatles were as much a revolutionary force as any charismatic leader and their effect was a profound one which changed our cultural as well as our musical perceptions. Despite the efforts of people like Otto, Weber and the two Neumanns, we still only dimly understand the phenomenon of charismatic individuals like Dean and know even less about the numinous quality they possess. In the realm of popular culture it is this numinous quality which above all separates the great popular artist — the pop icon — from the run-of-the-mill. Elvis Presley had it. Bessie Smith had it. Certainly Louis Armstrong had it. The Beatles had it. While some people believe we can describe much of popular art as formula — taking the lead from John Cawelti's brilliant essays and his book *The Six-Gun Mystique* — it is the numinous quality in these popular artists which resists formulation and makes popular art so interesting. For Cawelti, "formula stories . . . are structures of narrative conventions which carry out a variety of cultural functions in a unified way. We can best define these formulas as principles for the selection of certain plots, characters, and settings which possess in addition to their basic narrative structure the dimensions of ritual, game, and dream that have been synthesized into the particular patterns of plot, character and setting which have become associated with the formula."[10] Understanding the formula will to some extent help us understand those who go beyond formula. The concept does not, however, help us understand the numinous quality of our pop idols. Formula tells us not what a popular artist's power is but what it is not. If all popular music, for instance, were mere formula then the record companies could predictably package one string of hits after another. They do this often enough, that's for sure; but every once in a while someone comes along who creates that special magic. Then we enter the realm of the numinous and they enter the Valhalla of pop iconography.

In that realm of the numinous, performer and audience do not need words to describe their mutual sharing of magic — as the behavior of the Beatles' concert goers shows so well. The attraction shared is not unlike that which one finds in charismatic leaders and their movements and mass rallies. The numinous performer and the charismatic leader have more in common than most of us care to admit. Yet if we could understand more of the nature of this quality in pop idols we might also come to a greater understanding of the power of a Hitler.

Looking back on the Beatles' reign as pop heroes, I believe that a great deal of their magic came from their talent as comedians. In fact they may well have been the greatest comedians since Chaplin. (In light of my previous comments about the numinous qualities of pop stars and charismatic leaders there is that curious relationship between Chaplin and Hitler — Hitler looked like Chaplin, Chaplin parodied Hitler in *The Great Dictator*.) Like Chaplin they were masters of timing and mimicry. There is even a parallel in their work — the early shorts, Chaplin's film *The Circus* and *Sgt. Pepper*, the *White Album* and *Modern Times*. (I have always thought of the *White Album* as a time capsule — a collection of observations about the world at that time.) Like Chaplin, the Beatles had a vision behind their work — an affirmation of the humanity of us all, a belief in freedom in its fullest sense and above all a spirit of fun. Like Chaplin's, the Beatles' vision sometimes slipped into sentimentality — in fact the same kind of winning sentimentality that Chaplin had. The audiences who left *Yellow Submarine* singing "All You Need Is Love" were not unlike the audiences who left *Modern Times* humming "Smile."

In the tradition of Chaplin and other truly great popular artists the Beatles were powerful because they were at once so different and yet so much like all of us. (Historians have speculated that this was also Hitler's great appeal.) Just as we all could see something of ourselves in Chaplin's little tramp, so the collective individuality of the Beatles fits those pop stereotypes that are deeply ingrained in all of us: Ringo, the folksy "good old boy," Paul, the teenage heart throb; John, the irreverent whippersnapper; George, the quiet intellectual who as some put it must be "deep." Each of them said things people wanted to say but couldn't. They put down all the pretensions of modern life. Chaplin's famous kick in the pants — the thing we all wanted to do to some pompous personage — was as much as the basis of the Beatles' humor as it was Chaplin's. When their own pretensions were getting a bit thick, the Beatles were not above poking fun at themselves just as Chaplin could do so well.

Coupled with their collective identities, the Beatles brought with them a great sense of timing. As with Chaplin the essence of their timing was the use of the unexpected. Certainly one of the most remarkable things about the Beatles' icon was how it varied.

The phrase that so many people uttered back then — "growing up with the Beatles" — was not an idle phrase, for perhaps unique among pop icons the Beatles ranged across all facets of twentieth-century music and created for us an amazing stew full of heady ingredients. They were constantly surprising us with their inventiveness. If Cawelti is right about the essence of popular art being convention and given in extreme cases the rote repeating of the same patterns, then the Beatles were superb — in the sense of being above — popular art, for they took the conventions, mixed them in that fabulous stew of theirs and produced works that turned the conventions back on themselves or went beyond them. Space, time, language, musical styles were mixed so freely they became irrelevant. Andre Bazin once said the essence of Chaplin's comedy lay in his irreverent use of objects — remember the immortal scene of Chaplin eating his shoe in *The Gold Rush*? So the essence of the Beatles' music was their irreverent use of the conventions of popular music. Chaplin eating his shoe left one laughing and crying at the same time, the same feeling one gets from songs like "Happiness Is a Warm Gun" or "Maxwell's Silver Hammer." "Maxwell's Silver Hammer" is the food-feeding machine gone mad in *Modern Times* or in the same film the crazy Charlie tightening the buttons on a woman's dress with his wrenches.

As Chaplin helped us get through the twenties and thirties so the Beatles helped us get through the sixties. The sixties — two decades compressed into one — first the wild free times then the times of

147

social upheaval. In the end both were superseded by evil not even their comedy could exorcise, (Spencer Bennett in an article "Christ, Icons and Mass Media" pointed to the Beatles' role of exorcism: "They have been molded as exorcisers of society by media just as Jesus was given stature by the Church as healer in iconographic form."[11]). Chaplin submerged by Hitler and the American McCarthyite fascists, the Beatles by Nixon, their song "Revolution" seeming a tame message after the deaths at Kent State. Black comedy became the style. Whimpy Mick Jagger singing "Street Fighting Man" seems a bit silly now but it was all the rage then as thousands of middle-class white college students who had never been closer to the streets or a fight than the nearest TV set donned fatigue jackets and Chairman Mao caps and exclusive dress shops sold cartridge belts to debutantes all bent on bringing about revolution. Such earnest figures, whether they be pseudo-revolutionaries, the ad men and lawyers who surrounded Nixon, or the stormtroopers and assorted deviants who surrounded Hitler are beyond comedy. (My father who escaped from Germany in the thirties said he thought *The Great Dictator* wasn't really that funny at the time, because Hitler couldn't be parodied.) You can laugh at cartoon Blue Meanies but the real ones are more deadly and no so humorous.

In considering the demise of the Beatles it is pertinent to remember that icons are above all objects. They can be plain and everyday or beautiful and unusual in their own right, but still they are only objects. These plain everyday objects do not become icons until we endow them with those other-worldly qualities that we ourselves find necessary to give them. The qualities we choose and the reasons we choose them are as varied as all the vagaries of human nature.

So it was with four plain lads from Liverpool, each — as John Lennon put it — an individual in his rite. Collectively they became the Beatles and we made a cultural icon of them. For awhile they threatened to outshine even the most sacred of the old icons — remember when it was said that the Beatles are bigger than Christ? The Beatles made the remark themselves at a press conference. To some it was blasphemous while to others it was a part of a press conference put-on, which stars like Dylan cultivated and whose precursors were the conferences given by idols like James Dean and Chaplin. The remark, though, was a bit more complex and profound than that. It illuminated the secular, popular nature of our society in a sudden dramatic way which hundreds of scholarly and not-so-scholarly articles could scarcely duplicate. In another way it alluded to the numinous quality the Beatles radiated for they did seem to possess something given to them by contact with what Rudolf Otto called "mysterious tremendum." This relationship with the other worldly is something many would dismiss as sheer crap, but David Dalton was perhaps closer to the truth than he realized when he spoke of James Dean as a modern Osiris: "It is through our eyes that we have taken Jimmy into ourselves, and he remains there magically present like Osiris, god of regeneration."[12]

Perhaps if we are to search for formula and conventions in figures like Dean and the Beatles we would do well to look at religious and charismatic archetypes. Dalton's brilliant insight could open the door to a whole area of cultural investigation which would serve to begin to illuminate the numinous side of our psyches: a revival of Otto's attempt on a secular level. As a beginning of such an attempt maybe we should differentiate between popular, political and religious charisma. It also might be more useful to refer to all these figures as charismatic icons to differentiate them from Fishwick's objective icons. Unlike those medieval icons which were paintings and objects, the Beatles were four living human beings. Ultimately they could not live as a collective idea and once again became mere mortals. Unlike Jimi Hendrix, Jim Morrison, Janis Joplin, and a host of burned out blues musicians, they at least were able to live with their humanity. That they are now less than perfect is not without its satisfaction.

In this light I wonder why so many of our charismatic icons die such untimely deaths. Even Hemingway — at once the strongest and the most vulnerable — succumbed. Those that do not die untimely deaths become sickening parodies of themselves like Elvis had become or like Mick Jagger is well on his way to becoming. The easy answer is that they could not live up to their own hype. No doubt there is a great deal of truth to that but it is still too simple. The fate of the human beings we choose to elevate to the status of charismatic icons reminds me more of the archetypal ritual Sir James Frazier described in his study *The Golden Bough*. In Frazier's story there was a ritual slaying of the old king by a newer and younger one. Reading Frazier's story one's mind conjures visions of two men in jaguar skins, bedecked with jewelry and gold fighting to the death under the ritual tree. Cultures like to create their charismatic icons, endow them with magic and mystery (perhaps send them on tour), and then find they must slay them because they're so heavy. The Beatles realized this as much as anyone when they wrote "Sexy Sadie" or "When I'm Sixty-Four" — and still they were caught in the trap. Luckily today's pop idols are not destroyed in ritual fights to the death, although the game and the results can be as deadly. All charismatic idols — like Frazier's old king — know their time is limited. The determination of that time is based on popular mood and on the appearance of a new challenger. When the inevitable happens their popular identity will be destroyed. If they become too wrapped up in that popular identity then death can become quite literal. So they burn the candle at both ends with sometimes fatal consequences. Jim Morrison's "Light My Fire" with that awful line "and our love becomes a funeral pyre" summarized the relationship between the pop star/icon and the audience.

NOTES

[1]Marshal Fishwick and Ray Browne, eds., *Icons of Popular Culture*, (Bowling Green, Popular Press, 1970, p. 1.

[2]*Ibid., p. 4.*

[3]Jann Wenner, *Lennon Remembers*, N.Y., 1971, p. 84.

[4]Erich Neumann, *Art and the Creative Unconscious* (N.Y.: 1966), p. 97.

[5]Rudolf Otto, *The Idea of the Holy* (N.Y.: 1958).

[6]Franz Neumann, *Behemoth: The Structure and Practice of National Socialism*, (N.Y.: 1966).

[7]David Dalton, *James Dean: The Mutant King*, (N.Y.: 1975) p. 375.

[8]*Ibid.*, pp. 377 & 379.

[9]Max Weber, *On Charisma and Institution Building*, Chicago 1968, S.N. Eisenstadt, ed., pp. 19-20, 22.

[10]John Cawelti, "The Concept of Formula in the Study of Popular Culture," *Journal of Popular Culture* III:3, Winter, 1969, p. 390.

[11]*Icons of Popular Culture*, p. 10.

[12]Dalton, p. 373. A lengthy comparison of Dean and Osiris appears on pp. 370-373. Dalton's book is full of intuitive insights of this sort and is highly recommended to anyone studying the power of popular charisma.

FURTHER READING
PART III

The article that launched the serious study of the Beatles appeared in the London *Times* (December 27, 1963, page 4). Titled "What songs the Beatles sang," the piece was a favorable critique of their first two albums and made the first reference to "aeolian cadence." Such sophisticated terminology to describe rock-and-roll was at least three years ahead of its time, but the critic concluded: "They have brought a distinctive and exhilarating flavour into a genre of music that was in danger of ceasing to be music at all."

"The Music of the Beatles," from the *New York Review of Books* (January 18, 1968, pages 23–27), is a frequently reprinted appraisal by composer Ned Rorem. It has also appeared in *London Magazine* (February 1968, pages 54–64, under the title "America and the Beatles"), *The Beatles Book* (Cowles Education Corporation, 1968, here called "Why the Beatles Are Good") and *The Age of Rock* (Vintage Books, 1969). Mr. Rorem hails the coming of the Beatles as the most important event in music since the start of the previous decade.

Available from University Microfilms International, Ann Arbor, Michigan, are two dissertations on the music of the Beatles, *The Music of the Beatles from 1962 to "Sergeant Pepper's Lonely Hearts Club Band,"* by Terence J. O'Grady (Ph.D. University of Wisconsin-Madison, 1975) and *Rhythm and Harmony in the Music of the Beatles*, by Stephen C. Porter (Ph.D., City University of New York, 1979). O'Grady offers a musical analysis by year, illustrating the development of their style, ending in 1967. Porter places the Beatles in historical context after tracing the development of popular music, especially in America, from the 1700s to the 1950s. As they were written for an academic audience, both are challenging reading for the reader with no technical background in music.

A more readable work in the same vein is *Twilight of the Gods* (The Viking Press, 1973, paperback edition from Schirmer Books), by University of York, England, music professor Wilfred Mellers.

Mellers defines "aeolian" and "cadence" and combines his superior musical analysis with an explication of the Beatles' lyrics, recognizing them as both composers and poets.

The Beatles are treated solely as poets in *Things We Said Today* (The Pierian Press, 1980), by Colin Campbell and Allan Murphy. The most ambitious work concerning the Beatles' lyrics, it contains a compilation of and a concordance to the lyrics from all songs both written *and* recorded by John Lennon, Paul McCartney, George Harrison, and Ringo Starr as members of the Beatles.

Part IV
Two Movies

Introduction to
A HARD DAY'S KNIGHTS

Perhaps *New York Times* film critic Bosley Crowther surprised many readers when he compared (in the August 16, 1964, *Times*) the Beatles' "rapid-fire" and "sophisticated" first motion picture to a Marx Brothers comedy. Deemed superior to previous youth musicals, especially the films featuring Elvis Presley, "A Hard Day's Night" received widespread critical acclaim upon its release in 1964. In "A Hard Day's Knights," Jonathan Cott toys with the intellectual implications of Beatlemania on film.

The essay first appeared in *Ramparts*, October 1965, under the title "She Takes a Trip Around the World: A Hard Day's Night." (Cott's original title was "She Takes a Trip Around the World: A Hard Day's Knights.")

A HARD DAY'S KNIGHTS

by Jonathan Cott

INTRODUCTION

"Come Balthazar, we'll hear that song again."
—*Don Pedro in* Much Ado About Nothing

The surprise of the Beatles' film is that you need to see it again and again. A friend of mine met a WAC who had seen it fifty-two times: she was standing in the lobby of a movie theater, waiting out the second bill for her fifty-third epiphany. I have seen *A Hard Day's Night* five times and I will see it again. What does my, and perhaps your, repetition-compulsion mean? One watches great films like *Ivan the Terrible (Part II), Day of Wrath, Pickpocket, Rules of the Game* many times. The Bogart, Mae West, and Tarzan fans remain entranced with their idols after innumerable viewings. And films of negligible quality such as *One Eyed Jacks* have their devotees: one friend has seen the Western twelve times. But the *Hard Day's Night* syndrome is hardly cultish or eccentric. The second-run showings are usually packed with persons seeing the film for the third or fourth time. It is not unusual for you to return to one of the great films three or four times when you consider their technical quality and emotional power and your newer awareness of this power. But there is a law of diminishing returns here; after the fourth viewing of Becker's *Nightwatch* of Olmi's *The Fiancés*, you rest for a while before you return. I suppose you need them just so much, even as you realize their magnificence. The question is: why do we need *A Hard Day's Night* so much that we keep showing it as often as we do?

NAKEDNESS

Undrape! you are not guilty to me, nor stale nor discarded,
I see through the broadcloth and gingham whether or no,
And am around, tenacious, acquisitive, tireless,
and cannot be shaken away.
                    —Whitman, "Song of Myself"

On hearing the girls' screaming, you would imagine that the gods of fire, dawn, night, and thunder were manifesting themselves: "Let us adore this Wind with our oblation." But the girls scream so that they do not tear the Beatles' clothes off, for by screaming they alert the police who in turn set cordons up to block them from their desire. The Beatles have come running from the Garden: "I heard Thy voice in the garden, and I was afraid, because I was naked; and I hid myself." The girls think Adam's words. They are naked under their sweaters and skirts and desire to become one flesh with the un-dressed Beatles. So they are ashamed of this desire and scream loudly enough to be enjoined from their wish.

A Hard Day's Night tempts us with the excruciating hope that, when we see the film again, this time, surely, we shall see the four boys naked.

CHILDHOOD AND DEPENDENCY

When the world is reduced to a single dark wood
for our four eyes' astonishment,
—a beach for two faithful children,
—a musical house for our pure sympathy,
—I shall find you.
                    —Rimbaud, "Illuminations"

Childhood is our goal. Concomitant with being a child exists the pleasure one gets from playing and the intolerable displeasure one gets from realizing one's dependency on others. Thus the Beatles play on the rugby field in that most pleasurable scene which you want to see again and again. Four boys mock space and time — the sequence lasts under three minutes — as they play to "Can't Buy Me Love." Every moment seems spontaneous and joyful. Actions and movements are speeded up and slowed down. What we see is how we truly wish we felt or remember how we once felt or how we once wanted to feel. "Genital organization is a tyranny in man because his peculiar infancy has left him with a lifelong allegiance (i.e., fixa-tion) to the pattern of infantile sexuality" (Norman O. Brown). If this is correct, why does the playing terminate? After that beautiful

158

scene of exhaustion when the Beatles — lying on the grass, hands under their heads — count or talk silently to themselves? The answer is that 1) Mr. Genital Reality orders them off his field; and that 2) the Beatles have a TV rehearsal waiting for them. They have escaped from their duties: no job, no "Money" — which song comments obversely on that working-day world situation which "Can't Buy Me Love" attempts to fantasize away. The balding TV director ("It's a young man's business") depends on the manager who depends on the Beatles who depend on both, even when they do not wish to admit it. When Ringo gets led astray by the clean old id man, he assumes independence, and, in the tramp sequence, appears comic to us — the Bergsonian object-butt — but we have lost our goal, we laugh at the child in us now. The jokes are on Ringo, but he does not enjoy them. For the Beatles are boys, not bums, and they try their best not to "grow up."

REACHING OUR GOAL
OR GOODBYE TO BEAUDELAIRE'S OWLS

Such was that happy Garden-state
While man there walked without a mate.
—Marvell, "The Garden"

Thus *A Hard Day's Night* does not, in Keats' words, unperplex bliss from pain; still, it strives honorifically towards our longed-for goal of childhood by focusing on the four boys in action. The great Sung neo-Confucianist philosopher Chu Hsi wrote: "Nature is the state before activity begins, the feelings are the state when activity has started . . . . " The verb "to act," in fact — which, in a general sense, means "to begin," "to lead," and eventually "to rule" (from the Greek *archein*) and also "to put in motion" (from the Latin *agere*) — suggests the Beatles' style of life. Their actions and their songs are impelled not from what they know but from what they are — from feelings rather than from states of mind. Boys and girls are naturally active, and it takes a bit of acculturation before they become bored, depressed, and hung-up. Talking at press conferences, taking a bath, dancing, singing, playing cards, running in and out of jail (even the car thief and the cops become game-playing boys again — society's standards are demolished) — all these actions are invested with pleasurable feeling. The Beatles need only themselves for their own resources. Most important is the fact that each Beatle makes an idea of himself; and that is why we suddenly realize in amazement that the Beatles sing love songs like "If I Fell" and "I Only Want to Dance with You" only to themselves. "You" means "me" in these songs. There is no "other," but they can say "we" to themselves

159

and to each other. The Beatles' state of nature — to refuse Chu Hsi for a moment — is just this state of self-idealized and self-absorbed activity. The Beatles pinch chorus girls backstage, they get married, but that is, as Gatsby said, "merely personal." It doesn't matter. The Beatles' songs are full of feeling because the Beatles like to sing; but it is the singing that is important, for the "feeling" is the state when the singing has started. The girls are screaming, but, as one of the pupils of Heraclitus said perhaps, is this screaming not part of the song?

LOVE

" . . . . dearest M / please come.
There is no one here at all."

—Robert Creeley

The Beatles love what they do, so they love themselves. The screaming girls love the Beatles, and the Beatles are the receptacle or container of their love. They also resemble the Greek god of love, in the sense that Kierkegaard speaks of him:

> It is a genuine Greek thought that the god of love is not himself in love, while all others owe their love to him. If I imagined a god or goddess of longing, it would be a genuinely Greek conception, that while all who knew the sweet unrest of pain or of longing, referred it to this being, this being could know nothing of longing.

But the Beatles not only embody love, they are the Incarnation of Love. As Kierkegaard writes:

> In the Incarnation, the special individual has the entire fullness of life within himself, and this fullness exists for other individuals only in so far as they behold it in the incarnated individual. (From *Immediate Stages of the Erotic*)

The Beatles are as extraordinary as they are because they not only represent Love but also contain the "entire fullness" of Love within themselves. They are thus an embodiment and container of Love, and they are also the Love which they contain. There is no one there at all but themselves.

PHYSICALITY

Should time be gone,
and all that is impermanent a mere lie?
—Nietzsche, "Thus Spake Zarathustra"

It has been observed that *A Hard Day's Night* is not strong on plot. This is of course true. But it is not jokes — "campy," anti-Nazi, anti-cops — as good as they are that hold your interest. Rather it is the director's total dependence on showing the physical immediacy of the events and persons observed that generates the film's excitement and pleasure. I can think of no major feature film other than Dreyer's *Passion of St. Joan* that emphasizes the physical fact in such an unmitigated fashion. In Dreyer's film, the fly on Joan's eye, the warts on the interrogator's face, the cripples hanging around, the child sucking the mother's breast just when Joan, about to die, says: "Where will I be tonight?" — all these observed events heighten Dreyer's outraged sense of the flesh, all the more heightened as they contrast with Joan's saintliness. And yet her face, revealing all the confusion and suffering, is the most excruciating of physical facts.

The Beatles' faces and the parts of their faces, however, are the exultantly observed images — if not the heroes — of *A Hard Day's Night*: eyes, noses, hair, teeth. The image of a hand caressing a guitar, first seen on the studio's TV screen, is as close to suggesting a sense of sexual love as the film allows and so eerily reverberates with more force than had it been employed in a different context — say in an Italian comedy, where everyone is touching. The surprise and exhilaration you feel is similar to how you feel at that beautiful moment in Kurosawa's *High and Low* when you first see the kidnapper in his white clothes — as if he were a princess — reflected in the stream of the Tokyo slum.

Then, too, there are the faces of the girls and women. Their faces reveal as much about them as the humors reveal the characters in Jonson's plays. Just a second's sight of them unimaginably expresses the essence of girlhood. As the Beatles sing on TV, you see the girls in the audience, eyes dilating, each one unique from any other in her ecstasy and the force of her early but veritable sexuality. And if the girls seem womanly, the women seem girlish: the wonderfully shy creature talking to Ringo at the press conference, the women dancing at the party, the sexy secretary putting on her shoes who leads George into the shirt designer's office. The Beatles enable the women to become girls; the girls, women — even if only for a moment or the length of a song.

ROCK AND ROLL MUSIC, OR AT CH'U HILL WHEN THE RIVER STOOD STILL

And we sail on, away, afar,
Without course, without a star,
But, by the instinct of sweet music driven;

161

Till through Elysian garden islets
By thee, most beautiful of pilots,
Where never mortal pinnace glided,
The boat of my desire is guided:
Realms where the air we breathe is love,
Which in the winds and on the waves doth move,
Harmonizing this earth with what we feel above.
      —Shelley, "Asia's Song" *from Prometheus Unbound*

Let us take a roundabout path by examining a beautiful ancient Chinese folk song:

> I heard my love was going to Yang-chow/and went with him as far as Ch'u Hill./For a moment, when you held me fast in your out-stretched arms/I thought the river stood still and did not flow.

The sense of stillness and gentleness of the poem's statement brings out the superficial stillness of the emotion the girl says she feels. For there is no sense of passivity here. Rather, the mind and its experiences have been undifferentiated and everything is bursting out from a single source. The past and future combine, with time superseded, so that the present moment becomes eternal. Everything which is flowing remains rooted in this eternal present so that the stillness she feels, while everything is flowing within that stillness, is a bliss and joy that cannot be expressed, only suggested, which this song does so magnificently. Rock and roll songs almost always last under three minutes. The Beatles' songs, like most rock and roll songs, do not develop their musical materials in the way that the sonata-allegro form develops them or in the way that contemporary serial works develop them through permutation. The simple employment of the diatonic scale, usually two themes, and the relatively uncomplicated chord progressions limit development. (The Beatles' songs hint slyly at modal melodic patterns, but they too are diatonic.) Now the reality of Eternity can be felt only in that paradoxical moment of time when time has been superseded so that the present moment becomes eternal. The limited and limiting musical materials out of which rock and roll is created are perfectly suited to the demands of one's perception of Eternity. Everything in the song — in spite of the strophic tension which is undercut or neutralized by means of the continual 4/4 beat — enables you to remain rooted in the eternal present, so that the "river" does in fact stand still.

In this ambience of three-minute timelessness, we are taken outside of ourselves, if we allow ourselves to be so taken. We are taken back to the Garden where the "tragicomedy of love is performed by

162

starlight" and the fireworks light up the sky. It is the blissful peace of the Diamond Samadhi where you feel, like a gentle rain, the soft petals of multi-colored lotus blossoms and those inexplicable, crazy feelings spreading throughout your gums.

Rock and roll is the new mysticism for those too experienced and cynical to believe much in anything anymore — a mysticism which you can accept for three minutes, a veritable even if non-interpersonal giving of oneself, because there is no fear of losing out. (There is here, too, also a return to the undifferentiated world of early childhood experiences.)

The hard day's night, the race to the train, the playing and singing — this is the passion of the world. But in the end, the Beatles in their helicopter fly up to Heaven. Is this not the Easter revelation we all have need of re-experiencing? *A Hard Day's Night* combines radical innocence and religious revelation, inviting ecstasy and salvation to that soul Yeats wrote about: "self-delighting, self-appeasing, self-affrighting"; whose "own sweet will is Heaven's will." Seeing the film again and again, we are the Vulture King seeing Rama in *The Holy Lake of the Acts of Rama:*

> As he went on, he saw the Vulture King lying on the ground, meditating on Rama's feet and the marks they bore. Raghubir, the ocean of grace, stroked his head with his lotus hands, and when he looked on the wondrous beauty of Rama's face, he felt no more pain.

OF THE COMFORT OF THE RESURRECTION
"Bring this boy into the world,
and we'll soon make another."
—Grandgousier in Rabelais' "Gargantua and Pantagruel"

The Beatles have made another film!

Introduction to
SCENARIOS FOR
THE REVOLUTION IN PEPPERLAND

"Once upon a time, or maybe twice, there was an unearthly paradise called Pepperland. Eighty thousand leagues beneath the sea it lay. Or lie, I'm not too sure."

Thus began the epic voyage of the Yellow Submarine in the 1968 animated feature "Yellow Submarine." In "Scenarios for the Revolution in Pepperland," David Bowman traces the journey of the submarine, both the real adventure of its creators, designer Heinz Edelmann, producer Al Brodax and writer Erich Segal, and the imagined trip of its cartoon crew, the Beatles.

SCENARIOS FOR
THE REVOLUTION IN PEPPERLAND

by David Bowman

(an unguided tour of *The Yellow Submarine*, the animation industry, and the state of our Piscean world)

> *We shouted to the soldiers, 'Join us! Join us!' We believed that they might throw off their helmets and come to our side. We had girls, pot, food, community warmth, and weren't taking any orders. They were all regimented and controlled. It was the psychedelic vs. the linear, free vs. fixed, spontaneous vs. uptight. (Jerry Rubin,* Do It!*)*
>
> *Hallo there, blue people. Won't you join us? Hook up, and otherwise commingle. (John,* The Yellow Submarine*)*

A week ago I happened to be reading Jerry Rubin's account of the Battle of the Pentagon, Oct. 21–22, 1967, while I was rolling a print of *The Yellow Submarine* at the Library of Congress. I saw that the film's final battle between the Beatles and the Blue Meanies was a scenario for the revolution.

But the film is revolutionary in style, too. And it is the great synthesis of revolutionary forces coming together during 1967–8, when the film was being made, especially the Beatles music, the anti-war movement, op-pop art, and the freaks and flowers the film was made for. Like the Beatles, *The Yellow Submarine* is greater than the sum of its parts, and deserves to be remembered.

The story of the making of the film starts not so much with Heinz Edelmann, its designers, as with the great artistic head who inspired him, Saul Steinberg. Steinberg used to say that the purpose of his drawings is to make people feel there is something else beyond the perception, that he is playing with the voyage between the perception and the understanding, and that his work is a riddle in the form of a drawing. *The Yellow Submarine* is a riddle in the form of thousands of drawings.

Remember Steinberg's *Labyrinth*, at the dark end of the Ike-and-Dick era, with its fezzy parade of Shriners, its crocodiles, which he says all artists have behind them when they work, its mortuarial Uncle Sams, its Flying Gloves, its rocket-propelled abstractions, and YES fighting NO on vast empty landscapes where anything is possible because nothing is real but drawn by hands which draw other hands?

It's all in *The Yellow Submarine*, images as well as ideas, doing their thermal dance through the nöosphere, where nothing is real or at rest or comprehensible to Euclid, Newton, or Disney, but you feel Heraclitus, Einstein, and Joyce would have loved it, without caring what reels were shown in what order, the bourgeois hangup of the projectionist. It is a truly international film, an Aquarian film, because it was inspired by the Beatles; designed by Heinz in Germany, himself inspired by a Hungarian in New York; animated by about six dozen Englishmen, Canadians, and Australians working in London; scripted and produced by Americans; and largely ignored by everyone except the admen, for whom it has been required viewing for about four years now.

The Yellow Submarine created a revolution in graphic style, the YES-style, and singlehandedly revived a dying animation industry, which had fallen between dismal imitation of the Disney Studios and the British flimsies, those funny little men with large noses and bowler hats who do whimsical things in the same droll way.

The idea for the film came in 1966 on the heels of a series of commercials using cartoon figures of the Beatles, part of them subcontracted to TV Cartoons, and George Dunning, who would direct *The Yellow Submarine*. Since the commercials were pretty horrible, everyone knew a new designer was needed. Charlie Jenkins, who did many of the finest parts of the film, suggested Heinz Edelmann, and that was that.

Charlie told me that King Features was "apprehensive, but nevertheless interested, simply because they were treading on new ground, and the first and foremost ambition was to make money. There they had the Beatles music, the rights to use it in animation — they got a plot from United Artists — and the money to do it, so they weren't going to fail by making it a picture for intellectuals."

King Features were rather bludgeoned into doing it the animators' way, because everyone in London ignored their doubts, and the thing progressed into a two-minute pilot film, "Lucy in the Sky with Diamonds," done by Bill Sewell. Lucy proved to be the keystone of the best King Features shown since their thirteen-part Flash Gordon serial done in the 1930's. "They got such a reaction to it," Charlie said, "like Americans do when they react, it was terrific, they had Lucy running constantly on a loop in the foyer of King Features."

The Americans were knocked out by their own stuff. Old stuff at that, from the Golden Age of Movies. Lucy was done with an animation technique devised by the Disney Studios back in the 1930's called rotoscoping, where live-action film is projected onto celluloid sheets, one frame at a time, then traced off, then painted various ways, then rephotographed like any ordinary animation. Disney had resorted to it for Prince Charming and Snow White so they would look like beautiful people, circa 1936, and not like pigs, mice, or dogs. The fact that they look like Frederick March and Ruby Keeler is coincidental, as is the fact that the Lucy sequence was rotoscoped from old Busby Berkeley clips of the same vintage.

"Eleanor Rigby," with its surrealistic street scenes of Liverpool, was another departure from Heinz' design; it was done by Charlie Jenkins and Sue Willis without the knowledge of King Features. "When they saw the thing they were horrified, and took an instant dislike to it, until the Sunday papers saw it and pointed out WOW this is like animated Warhol, so it soon became a terrific thing for the producer, Al Brodax to point out we were using Warhol, Picasso, Beardsley, Bridget Riley, it's all going into the film, we're using everything; we're swallowing up everything, it's all going in, you're getting great value for your money."

And they were. From then on, everyone got their own way, without being cautious, routine, or look-alike. It was a genuine attempt to experiment and it succeeded. This time no one had to worry about stuffy old clients, the Blue Meanies, or where the money would come from, because it was there with all the Beatles' magic, who saved the British cultural economy almost singlehandedly, or eighthandedly, without stopping to be thanked for it.

So Charlie did the title sequence, because it had to be done, at the last minute, and the Eleanor Rigby sequence, and the Northern Song sequence, but he also built the model for the Yellow Sub itself, and got all the trajectory work done for it, less artistic than servicing, because it had to be done.

"Northern Song" was a sequence of cubes, using posterized caricatures of Beatles faces, with some op-geometry applied, and a nonsense song, using an oscilloscope image integrated into it, just to break up the monotony for the people sitting in the audience.

The monotony of a cartoon feature is even more intense than the monotony of a live-action feature. Perhaps United Artists realized this when they billed it as 'animated live-action extravaganza.' So about six dozen artists knocked themselves out to keep it alive and as extravagant as possible. Everything was thrown in, integrated, artistically united, from one moment to the next: rotoscoping, multi-plane, photo-stenciled silk screen, polarizing filters, stills animation, cutouts, watercolor backgrounds, oscilloscopes, traveling mattes, live-action superimpositions, pixillations, EVERYTHING, plus op art, puns, parodies, private jokes, whimsies, and great gobs of nonsense.

Synthesis, the great synthesis, like the Beatles themselves, the whole greater than the sum of its parts, synergetics, or at least synthetics, but real synthetics, that do something good together, not the imitation plastic you pay $3 to see downtown.

Yet *The Yellow Submarine* is not a film, but a series of films, an anthology of animation, exciting for themselves, stickytaped together with Beatles music and a thin jokey storyline manufactured at the last minute of Erich Segal (author of *Love Story*, authority on classical Roman comedy, Ph.D., who parodied himself and his academic kind as the Nowhere Man, Jeremy Hillary Boob, Ph.D., "polyglot classicist, hard-biting satirist, good dentist, too") and by Segal's friends at King Features.

The film's sub-title, NOTHING IS REAL, means among other things that it's all in the mind, as we shall see, and that everything is disguised. The film can be read like the Book of Revelations, provided you have the keys to it drawn by the animators themselves. Its heroes are lovable freaks; its villains are lovable fascists.

The Blue Meanies have Mickey Mouse ears and Pluto ears, which makes them Disney Agents. They wear cowboy boots and spurs and robber masks, which makes them a bit like American agents of LBJ, circa 1967, and they are blue, the color of cops, jet jockeys, and tories, which makes them politically distinguishable from the Red Meanies. Their weaponry is unmistakably now, like the Anti-Music Missile, the glass balloon fired out of its underground silo to bag up Sgt. Pepper's Lonely Hearts Club Band; the Count Down Clowns, with their nose-cone nose and buttons lighting up like computer displays; the sinister Flying Glove, a heat-seeking missile which sends out red-and-yellow stripes from its blue body; and the other weaponry which blow away the trees, incinerate and defoliate the greenery, bleaching the color out of Pepperland and freezing its people, like an aerial Mace, dis-animating them and therefore destroying them.

At the head of the Meanies is the megalomaniac Chief Blue Meanie, said to be modeled on newsreels of Hitler (a safe thing to say) but wearing cowboy boots and spurs. Sometimes he shrieks and pulls his general lackey Max's beagle ears; sometimes he croons a soft Guy Lombardo phrase. "Hail to the Chief" is not played, but the CBM is as much LBJ as AH. In short, a thoroughly lovable villain.

The Meanies' legions include the Hidden Persuaders, bald business mafia who smoke cigars, wear double breasted suits, hold chalices with martini olive eyes, and shoot from their shoes, tanned Marshal Ky types in sunglasses, moustaches, olive drab tunics and high-braid hats; the fezzed Snapping Turtle Turks, with shark-snapping stomachs; squat little moneybag monsters numbered 1-2-3-4-5-

170

6-7-8-9-10; the people-stoning Apple Bonkers, who drop money-green apples on talent in Pepperland, because they are mortuarial Uncle Sams, and the money always comes out of the Big Apple — where the "petrified mountain spires" referred to in the film's original script are located.

At this point things get very iffy, like interpretations of Lewis Carroll's fantasies, which *The Yellow Submarine* at times very much resembles, as it resembles in other ways recent animation like Lenica's *Labyrinth*, Trnka's *Ruka*, or Borowcyzk's *Astronauts*. Still, guessing is irresistible.

Are the Kinky Boot Beasts reminders of the aggressive girl fans, in their kinky boots and Kings Road gear, who used to assault the Beatles and their wives?

Is Pepperland meant to be another Cockaigne, the land of idleness and plenty, identified with London, or is it Cocaine, pepper itself, the land of pleasant no feeling? Is 'Sgt. Pepper's Lonely Hearts Club Band' the band of British soldiers demobilized after their finest hour, doomed to finish out their days in pubs and pleasant idleness? Is this the meaning of the opening lines of the song that twenty years ago today, circa 1945, the band began to play?

Is this the reason for the Pepperlanders' period costumes from the not long ago Edwardian and Georgian eras, reminders of the good old days before the Americanization of England?

The year on the Yellow Sub dial says 2000, to date their Aquarian trip, then flips back to 1959, the year of Beatles to the rescue, then rolls back year-by-year (and frame-by-frame) to 1913. But when the Sub reverses itself in the Sea of Time, the years begin with 1919, roll forward to 1959, then return to 2000 and forward to the perilous future.

If *The Yellow Submarine* means anything besides mindless entertainment, the meaning is here, in Pepperland sinking beneath the waves of economic imperialism, towards the year 2000, which animators have known and felt for many years as the wage-slaves of advertising. Pepperland speaks English; the Blue Meanies scream in American.

In fact, the Seven Seas the Beatles must get through are the horrors of an ad-mad world: THE SEA OF CONSUMER PRODUCTS, the pills to be pushed, THE SEA OF MUSIC, the sugar-coated jingle, THE SEA OF TIME, squeezing and stretching to fit air-time spots, THE SEA OF MONSTERS, the chimeras of crackbrained overstrained genius, THE SEA OF PHRENOLOGY, where head gears turn overtime, THE SEA OF HOLES, dreading noughts and losses, and THE SEA OF GREEN, in-rolling money.

The best monster they meet in these seas is the Vacuum Flask Monster, the vacuum tube of television, the voracious Box, which is

171

so voracious that it sucks up everything sooner or later, good and bad alike, disasters, commercials, old movies, reputations, privacy, death, music, and all of us, just to get itself through one week of air time.

Animators know that the Box sucks up commercials as fast as they can be made, but it does worse things. It bleaches out the art, for who among us sees their true colors, and it distorts the image, down to a few square inches called the Safe Image Area, outside of which all is lost in the furry-blurry.

Worst of all, the Box is absolutely impartial, egalitarian, latitudinarian, nondiscriminating, like social democracy. Its bad commercials sell just as well as its good commercials, maybe even better, and the Hidden Persuaders know this. So still employed are the funny little men, straight from the pages of *How to Draw Cartoons*, inspired by UPA figures like Mr. Magoo, himself drawn as a protest against the sanitized-deodorized Disney animals which we still think of as what animation should be.

So *The Yellow Submarine* is the animator's revenge, both a political and a personal statement, cleverly concealing the bites at the only hands feeding him these days. Since the cinema stopped buying animation, animators have had to succumb to the Blue Meanies, their hardware and their software. The way out for the Pepperlanders is to send for the Beatles to rescue them, and of course the Beatles do, by reviving animation as well as British exports, arts, and popular culture, and by inspiring *The Yellow Submarine* to be made.

But the YES-style is also a YES-mood, and YES coupled to LOVE in great block letters is what saves Pepperland from the Blue Meanies. All you need is LOVE, et cetera, and everything turns out right. It's all in the mind, y'know. It is manic, mind-expanding stuff, like Joyce,

LORD MAYOR: *Four scores and thirty-two bars ago our fore-fathers —*
FRED: *Quartet —*
LORD MAYOR: *And fore-mothers —*
FRED: *Another quartet —*
LORD MAYOR: *Made it, in this Yellow Submarine*
Einstein,
GEORGE: *What's happening, John?*
JOHN: *Well, in my opinion we've become involved in Einstein's time and space continuum theory.*
RINGO: *Oh, aye.*
JOHN: *Relatively speaking, that is.*
RINGO: *Maybe time's going on strike.*
PAUL: *What for?*

172

RINGO: *Shorter hours . . . there's a 24 hour day, isn't there?*
GEORGE: *Hey look. Everything's getting bigger.*
JOHN: *It's not. It's us that are getting smaller.*

and all in all like amphetamines, "causing profound psychic effects, wakefulness, and mental alertness, increased initiative and elevation in mood, euphoria or elation, lessened sense of fatigue, talkativeness, and increased ability to concentrate, especially on solving problems," which is at once a prescription for the ills of our Piscean world and the most concise review of the film, available not from a critic but from the *Encyclopaedia Britannica*, itself bought out by American money and shipped to Chicago.

Beyond the Americanization of Europe, beyond the Global Village, is the Age of Aquarius, when no ties of race or nation can keep people from brotherhood, unity, vision, and cooperation. *The Yellow Submarine* is an Aquarian fable made to warn us and to cheer us. It is a scenario for total revolution. John takes the word LOVE and smokes it. Everyone says YES and dresses as they want to. NO is replaced by KNOW. This is the world brain in action, ALL TO-GETHER NOW, in dozens of languages at the end of the film. This is Childhood's End, when everyone becomes a child, born again, under the sign of Aquarius, whose sign is wiggly waves, once water, now electricity. Pepperlanders are in fact Aquarians, the future race who live beneath the waves out of sight, saved by that relic of the Age of Pisces, the fishy Yellow Sub itself, perched on its pre-Columbian pyramid, blasted loose and propelled on a fishy odyssey in and out of Time, through the Seven Seas, before bringing back the Beatles to save Pepperland.

It is the Age of Aquarius when images pile up willy-nilly inside the Beatles house, faster than the eye can catch them, now you see it, now you don't, magic like Mandrake, beautiful like Marilyn, grotesque like Frankenstein, overwhelming like King Kong at the window. Ringo's car keeps changing color. George says it's all in the mind. They open the door and a locomotive speeds towards them. George says it's all in the mind.

When they reach the Sea of Phrenology — the foothills of the headlands, John says — they see into minds, a Steinbergian landscape, flashes of ERGO SUM, MAYBE, 1, H_2O, +/−, FREUD, DE SADE, A ROSE, E=MC^2, TRUE, in among flags, flowers, stars, emblems of all religions and nations, inside heads of all races, like Great Ideas of the World flashing past frame-by-frame too fast to grasp. Then we see in another head the psychedelic "Lucy in the Sky with Diamonds," with John as guide, a new Vergil, into the abyss of the five senses, Blake and Dante, but all in the mind, like the illusion of static images moving which is film itself.

This is the Age of Aquarius when mysticism arrives at the same dimensionless point as rational science, water flow and electron flow, through absurdities and apparent impossibilities, to the ultimate reality, when logical and astrological are neither more nor less than there, together, in among the stars, or whatever they are, the Sensorium Dei as Newton described it.

The signs of Aquarius are here already, in odd places like Houston, where the Manner Space Flight Center lies down with the Astrodome, where no wind blows and no grass grows, because the grass is plastic. All is not grass that astrograss, and the Astrodome looks like nothing so much as a flying saucer from astrospace.

Unless you spend millions, as Stanley Kubrick did on *2001: A Space Odyssey*, the only way to indulge in mind-expanding films is through animation, and the possibilities again become unlimited. Charlie Jenkins claims that cartooning is only 10% of animation; the other 90% is still waiting to be discovered through new designs, forms and techniques. So he's doing scan-animation and collaborating with David Bailey in animating transparencies. John Whitney and others are working with computer animation. Douglas Trumbull is elaborating the slit-scan process he used for the Stargate sequence in *2001*. And dozens of others around the world are doing wild new things that will be seen sooner or later.

The problem is always the money. Admen are the only people buying animation these days, so the results are cautious, routine, and look-alike, despite the large number of animation studios around the world. It could have been otherwise, as *The Yellow Sub* showed, a film so important it should be hung and running in the Museum of Modern Art, part of the international heritage and all that, because it made the great synthesis of all the best artistic thrusts of our time.

Animation lovers will have to wait a long time, however, given the impossibilities of staying between the Sea of Holes, financial disaster, and the Sea of Green, financial glut. As Charlie Jenkins says about his London studio, Trickfilm, one year the clients love animation, the next year they loathe it. Too much business means no time or energy to do your own thing; too little business means no money for doing it.

The problem is also complexities of budgets for animation, design, tracing, painting, camera, all in advance, nothing for cost overruns, forwarding one-half at the outset, one-half for delivery of the block prints. Labor is paid on an hourly basis, or as freelance piece-working — we'd love to take you home with us. There are union agreements, footdragging, slapdashing, slipshodding, and woolgathering — the girl with kaleidoscope eyes. Studios are up against heavy deadlines, meddlers at all levels, slow film labs, and personality clashes — I am the walrus. All this, and more, before the sounds of sea gulls, steam engines, gremlins, toads, explosions, and princesses get married up to the artwork and entertainment comes, followed or not by a word from our sponsor over two, live, cuddly children licking plastic ices. All for some seconds of sell.

So no chance for another cartoon feature. No cash for it and no one wants to do it anyway. Cartoon features can tie up a whole studio for years, and anyway they are too long, like epic poetry, and too intense, giving visual indigestion and glazed eyeballs. *The Yellow Submarine* will have to be the best and the last of them all. Even the Disney Studios have given up, preferring live-action family movies, put out by Buena Vista, not exactly good viewing, and making millions off Disneyland and Disney World.

Therefore let us remember the wild fine fun of *The Yellow Sub-Submarine*: remember the demonstration of how long sixty seconds is by animating each second with twenty-four frames; remember John's cosmological query that maybe we're all part of a vast Yellow Submarine fleet; remember the death of that speech which used to stir Englishmen to die for King and Country whenever *Henry the Fifth* was revived, when the Chief Blue Meanie says 'Once more into the breach, dear Meanies'; and remember the truly sub-versive passages about rallying the land to rebellion, since the whole world's being attacked.

Then let us remember that *The Yellow Submarine* is a sad film; because it shows an animated England in costumes before its finest hour, now passed; because it shows the Beatles together, artists united, instead of split up; and because its happy scenario for the world cannot possibly come true.

FURTHER READING
PART IV

Some people just cannot see "A Hard Day's Night" too many times. A good companion for them is *The Beatles in Richard Lester's A Hard Day's Night: A Complete Pictorial Record of the Movie* (Penguin Books, 1978), by J. Philip DiFranco. The book contains dialogue, illustrated with stills from the movie, and an interview with director Richard Lester.

A fine critique of the Beatles' first film can be found in *Magil's Survey of Cinema* (Salem Press, 1980, volume 2, pages 712–715). The entry, written by Timothy W. Johnson reviews the highlights of the movie considered by critic Andrew Sarris to be "the 'Citizen Kane' of juke-box musicals."

If "A Hard Day's Night" can be compared to "Citizen Kane," then "Yellow Submarine" can be compared to "Fantasia." In "The Beatles, a Good Non-Literary Education Under Forty" (from *A Year in the Dark, Journal of a Film Critic*, Random House, 1969), Renata Adler suggests that "Yellow Submarine" is the best argument for feature-length cartoons since the Disney classic that combined great music with sophisticated animation. Adler applauds the creators for drawing on young people's sources of cultural education, comic strips in particular. Pauline Kael, on the other hand, ends her criticism "Metamorphosis of the Beatles" (from *Going Steady*, Little, Brown and Co., 1970) by criticizing the creators for borrowing too much from pop art or, as she states it, "ravaging the art of the twentieth century."

Thirty-seven Beatles films are covered in chapter six of *Beatle Madness* (Manor Books, 1978), by Martin A. Grove. Quoting extensively from contemporary reviews, Grove surveys movies featuring appearances by and/or the music of the collective and the individual Beatles, John and Yoko's experimental films and two television specials ("The Beatles at Shea Stadium" and "Magical Mystery Tour").

Part V
Beatlemania in the Seventies

Introduction to
BEATLEMANIACS NEVER DIE
(BUT THEY SURE GET CARRIED AWAY)

If, as Vance Packard suggested in "Building the Beatle Image," any businessman has been stuck with a warehouse full of Beatle wigs, he can probably unload them at a convention of Beatles fans. In 1981, "Beatlefests" were held in New Jersey, Houston, Chicago, Los Angeles and New York City. The first were held in New York at the Hotel Commodore and in Boston at the Bradford Hotel in 1974. Lilith Moon here describes how fans got carried away at the Boston gathering, buying up memorabilia and artifacts at outrageous prices and booing hysterically at the mention of Yoko Ono's name. The fans' buying habits have not changed in subsequent years, although their opinions of certain Beatle wives have; a woman dressed as Yoko received an ovation in the Grand Ballroom of the Hyatt Regency at the 1981 Chicago "Beatlefest."

BEATLEMANIACS NEVER DIE
(BUT THEY SURE GET CARRIED AWAY)

by Lilith Moon

It's the First Annual Beatles' Convention, Magical Mystery Tour, and I'm standing in the lobby of the Bradford Hotel, Boston. For the last hour I've been watching five teenage girls in black tee-shirts ("Bring Back the Beatles," "The Beatles Forever") collecting signatures for a petition to keep John Lennon in the United States. In the center of the room, gaggles of lean boys wearing row on row of Beatles' buttons flash rare albums at each other and reach out to fondle LPs missing from their collections. A blind woman wearing a long, dayglo green dress with sparkling rhinestones spelling out "JOHN GEORGE PAUL RINGO" is jauntily whisked through the lobby on the arms of a friend. No one notices.

Inside the hotel's cavernous ballroom this Saturday afternoon, 20 metal folding tables have been filled with Beatles' records and memorabilia. A thousand Beatle devotees, most of them under 20, crush through each other or peer between bodies to get a better view of the merchandise. Money changes hands quickly and cheerfully.

Among the items: Bubble gum cards with the Beatles ($1); the Polish poster for *A Hard Day's Night* ($3.50); tie tacks with individual Beatles' faces ($2); tie clasps shaped like a guitar with Beatle faces where the hole should be ($1.50); 1964 Beatles concert book, black with purple border and casual photos of all four Beatles inside ($20); foreign and domestic magazines with stories on the Beatles (80 cents to $20, including the 1964 *TV Guide* at $3), and more.

At one table the former president of the Beatles' New York fan club is selling promo photos, once free, for $2 to $4. She is only parting with her dupes, she says, as she keeps her eyes on the frenzy of hands flipping through her collection. "I'll clear, let me see, $200 when it's over. Pretty good, since they didn't cost me anything, right?" She smiles and winks.

At another table, men and women are anxiously sifting through stacks of bootleg Beatles records at $4 each. At yet another table, I pick up a copy of the mimeographed Beatles' fanzine *Strawberry*

Fields Forever, and brush up on my Liverpudlian slang. I also find that a letter writer, for reasons known only to himself, is looking for "a list of George Harrison's childhood diseases." Off in the corners of the auditorium, small groups of people pull out singles carrying cases, bubble gum cards, press clippings, and start making individual trades.

Later in this weekend, there will be nine straight hours of Beatle films and promo clips (including *Magical Mystery Tour*, of which three prints, worth $50,000 each, exist), there will be a march on the State House to keep John Lennon in America, and there will be much admiring of each others' buttons. But right now, Joe Pope, 26-year-old organizer of the convention and publisher of *Strawberry Fields Forever*, is calling the room to order for an auction of rare Beatles' memorabilia. Among the items:

A lunch pail (without thermos) with the Beatles in bas relief and color, is gobbled up by a New York publicist for $25. "I'll use it as a pocket book," she explains. "It'll be just GREAT at cocktail parties!"

A pair of Beatles sneakers (size 7 ½, women's, the only sneakers at the convention) go for $25. *This Is Where It All Started*, a Metro LP of Tony Sheridan and the Beatles, is worth $20. A mobile display unit for record stores brings in $12.50.

"And now," says Joe, "what you've all been waiting for, and what most of you have never seen. You've heard about it. It's called 'The Butcher.' It's the original cover of *Yesterday and Today*. Only 100,000 were printed. Most were destroyed by Capitol. It was considered in bad taste. Some are under the new cover of the LP. But this copy is not steamed off, it's *the original*."

Gasps go up from the crowd.

"We have a minimum of $200 on this item," Joe says, "and . . . here it is!"

He holds up a jacket with the four Beatles, grinning from ear to ear, dressed in white smocks and fondling decapitated dolls and sides of blood-red beef.

"You'll notice," Joe says pointing to the cover, "that there is no record with this. We collectors take out the record because it leaves a circle mark on the cover. The cover is the important thing. Now do I have a bid?"

The room grows silent, then one lone hand is raised. It belongs to an acned adolescent boy. He gets "The Butcher" and the room erupts in applause. End of auction.

The seller of that last item is Wayne Rogers, jocular president of a bootleg company called Rock and Roll University. He looks dejected as he tells me "I didn't want to sell 'The Butcher.' My wife made me. I wanted to trade it for an Atco promo record, *Ain't She*

Sweet. There was one guy here who had it, but he didn't want to get rid of it. I make money from the bootlegs and the tapes. That's what my company does. Right now I'm collecting tapes from Dylan's tour. I trade to get them. But I also have a private collection and that 'Butcher' was in perfect condition. I hung it on my wall."

David Peel, sometime street singer and friends with John Lennon, shows me a demo tape of something called "Marijuana," which he then proceeds to sing. "Marijuana, marijuana, marijuana," he yells. "We want marijuana, BRING BACK THE BEATLES." I tell him the song seems very appropriate.

The room is cleared and cleaned. Before long, it's filled up again, this time to hear Murray the K, once known as the 5th Beatle.

"I'm going to give you the bad news first. The Beatles will never, repeat, never, get together again."

A groan, coupled with boos, goes up from the crowd. Murray, stuffed in khaki slacks and white cowboy shirt, waits for the noise to die down.

"Now that you have the bad news, let me fill you in on all the gossip. The biggest shocker I can lay on you is that Ringo and Maureen are going to be divorced."

Murmurs from the crowd.

"George made sure, while Ringo was away, that Maureen wasn't lonely."

More murmurs.

"And, John is seeing Yoko Ono."

Boos.

"You know, I'd like to see a picture of Yoko Ono with a couple of lines that said, Rasputin in drag. All you Yoko Ono fans, well, all I can say to you is, Up Yours!"

Wild cheers.

"I'd just like to say one thing, there has never been nor will there ever be anything to rival the Beatles."

Tumultuous applause.

Introduction to
BOOTING THE BEATLES

While posthumous albums like **Rock 'N' Roll Music** can help a young fan discover the Beatles for the first time, bootleg albums of unreleased material can help an older fan discover a Beatles that he might not have heard before.

BOOTING THE BEATLES

by Charles P. Neises

As Pablo Picasso created "Guernica," the dramatic mural depicting the destruction of a Spanish town by German bombers during the Spanish Civil War, he allowed friend and photographer Dora Marr to photograph the work in progress. The first of her photographs only slightly resembles the finished work. Elements are removed and added as the series shows Picasso piecing together a puzzle of images relating to the catastrophe. The sketches on the canvas change as the days progress and as the artist refines his vision. The final photograph shows the great mural as we know it today.

In the business of recorded music, the artist rarely allows his product to be heard before it is finished. The Beatles were no different; their albums are generally considered great works of popular art. They did, however, allow the listener moments to hear the workings of the recording studio behind the record. Many groups start recording a song with a count-off (one, two, three, four!), which is later removed from the tape, but Beatles producer George Martin left in the count-off to *I Saw Her Standing There* on their first album. False starts are dealt with in the same manner, but the LP **Rubber Soul** contains a false start in the song *I'm Looking Through You*. At times, alternate versions of a single song are recorded, one to be released and the other to be discarded, but the Beatles released both fast and slow (not to mention politically decisive and indecisive) versions of *Revolution*.

In fact, the Beatles planned the movie "Let It Be" to show how songs are written, practiced, refined and recorded in the studio. In one scene, Paul McCartney leads the band in a rehearsal of *Maxwell's Silver Hammer*, singing out the chord changes. In others, Ringo Starr plays the piano and sings a few early verses of *Octopus's Garden*, and George Harrison experiments with arrangements of *I Me Mine*. As in the Dora Marr photographs, the pieces fall into place until the final scene, of the concert on a London rooftop, resembles the final product, the **Let It Be** album. "Let It Be" is like the Marr photos in yet another way: it was produced with the initial approval and cooperation of the artists involved. It was authorized.

Unauthorized recordings (bootlegs) of the "Let It Be" sessions do exist, but listening to them is a bit like peeking at the sketches that Picasso locked in his attic or burned after completing "Guernica." It is not known if Picasso ever hid or destroyed sketches for his masterpiece; the reference was made for the sake of analogy, but tapes of the Beatles' unfinished songs and rehearsals were either locked in recording company vaults, pitched into recording company garbage cans or stolen, borrowed, or otherwise lifted to be copied and marketed. These bootlegs are not to be confused with counterfeit records, cheap copies manufactured to resemble actual releases and to trick unsuspecting buyers, but they are equally illegal.

The practice of selling unauthorized recordings of musical performances is as old as the recording industry itself.[1] Bootleg recordings of the Beatles, usually taken from concerts and live radio and television appearances, were available in the middle 1960s and now enjoy brisk sales at fan conventions, antique and memorabilia shows, and some record stores. Sold through mailorder catalogs by underground companies with unusual names and frequently-changed postal addresses, most bootlegs are priced comparably with authorized albums. But, recalling the difference between a bootleg and a counterfeit, the material contained on most bootlegs does not compete with that found on commercial releases.

Frequently bootlegged materials are concerts, interviews, and studio outtakes. Concert bootlegs are popular because the Beatles conducted three world tours in the mid-1960s and did not release a live album until 1977. Interviews are easily copied from radio and television appearances. In one famous and oft-bootlegged interview, John Lennon gives a preview of the song *Don't Let Me Down* by strumming a guitar and shouting "Don't let me down! Don't let me down! (clears his throat) Don't let me down! Don't let me down! Can't remember anymore. Don't let me down," finally ending with an off-key rendition of *Those Were the Days*. Studio outtakes are songs recorded in the studio but never released. Some are not released because of time limitations on albums, others are excluded because they are pitifully substandard.

Pitifully substandard is how many a bootleg sounds to the uninitiated. Sound levels can be uneven throughout a single disk, usually devoid of careful mixing. Some copies are several generations removed from the original tape and no sophisticated stereo can make them sound better. They are sometimes packaged only in white sleeves accompanied by photocopied liner notes which may or may not include an accurate list of song titles. Clearly, these records are not aimed at the mass market of normal record buyers. What normal record buyer would really want a recording of John Lennon clearing his throat and forgetting the words to *Don't Let Me Down*? Some otherwise normal record buyers amass collections of every possible Beatles album and then set out to find material available only on bootlegs; these collectors are the counterparts of art enthusiasts who want to see pictures taken of a masterpiece before it was finished.

Bootleg recordings of studio outtakes can serve as valuable documentations of a recording artist's method of creating his work. As Picasso's creative process can be seen in the Marr photographs, bootlegs of the "Let It Be" sessions provide insights not offered in the movie or the legitimate **Let It Be** album. One song, *No Pakistanis*, appears on several bootlegs of material from these sessions; the version discussed here is found on a record titled **Sweet Apple Trax**. *No Pakistanis* is actually *Get Back* sung with lyrics concerning the unpopular immigration of Puerto Ricans to the United States and Pakistanis to England. The second verse ends with the line "don't want no Pakistanis taking all the people's jobs." Clearly anti-Pakistani, the exhortation "get back! Get back to where you once belonged" is here not friendly advice to a man in California or to a transvestite named Loretta, as it is in the authorized version of *Get Back*, but a stinging attack on dark-skinned immigrants.

Several clues suggest that *No Pakistanis* is an early version of *Get Back*: the arrangement is crude and the singer (Paul) mumbles the verses and improvises an instrumental solo by barking into the microphone. On the recording studio sketchpad of the tape machine, the group probably worked on the song, exercising enough good taste to omit the potentially offensive lyrics. What is left for the Beatles to perform on the authorized album is *Get Back*, stripped of its racial connotations, leaving only the Muslim name "Jojo." It is possible, however, that *No Pakistanis* is a put-on, recorded as a satire on the already written *Get Back*. But the Beatles were known to enter the recording studio with only a collection of incomplete songs. *A Day in the Life* (from the LP **Sergeant Pepper's Lonely Hearts Club Band**) was created using a song with no middle section by John and a short ditty by Paul as the middle section. Also on **Sweet Apple Trax** are unreleased songs titled *White Power* and *Back to Commonwealth*, both of which reflect the white-man's-burden tone of *No Pakistanis*.

The use of bootlegs like **Sweet Apple Trax** in the study of the Beatles' music is apt to increase as the group itself grows in musical and historical nature. With the release of **Sergeant Pepper's Lonely Hearts Club Band**, the Beatles launched themselves into the world of serious music, or so it would seem from the material published in the "serious" journals of the day. Their work was suddenly deemed suitable for discussion on the pages of *Partisan Review* and the *New York Review of Books*, and they became the subject of several Ph.D.

dissertations.[2] The road to artistic immortality is long, but the Beatles are well on their way, as a new generation of young record buyers, to whom the group might have seemed as dated as Rudy Vallee and Al Jolson, are discovering anew **Abbey Road, Rubber Soul, Revolver** and other great Beatles albums.

If, as discussed above, the "Let It Be" movie, showing the Beatles at work on an album, is the recording industry's equivalent to Dora Marr's photographs of "Guernica," then the studio outtake bootlegs[3] might someday take their places next to Leonardo DaVinci's notebooks. Like the outtakes, DaVinci's notebooks, with his mysterious code-like backward handwriting, were obviously intended for no audience but the artist himself. The surviving notebooks, however, are scrutinized by historians and are valued at millions of dollars each. Perhaps it is not presumptuous or pretentious to compare a rock-and-roll group with Picasso and DaVinci. Perhaps it is only premature.

NOTES

[1] See *You Can't Do That* (Pierian Press, 1981) by Charles Reinhart not only for its exhaustive index of Beatles bootlegs but for its appendix, an article ("Everything You Always Wanted to Know About Bootlegs, But Were Too Busy Collecting Them to Ask: A Treatise on the Wages of Sinning for Sound") by Tom Schultheiss detailing the history and present legal status of bootleg records.

[2] Terence J. O'Grady (Ph.D., University of Wisconsin–Madison, 1975) used bootlegs of early live performances to prepare his dissertation *The Music of the Beatles from 1962 to "Sergeant Pepper's Lonely Hearts Club Band."*

[3] See Reinhart's bootleg discography for a complete list of titles.

Introduction to
MAGICAL HISTORY TOUR

In this essay, Jerry Lazar reviews the state of Beatles collecting in the late 1970s. Displaying the gems of his collection (copies of George Harrison's LP **Wonderwall Music** and John and Yoko's LP **Two Virgins**), he surveys a few of the newer collectibles, both bad (a double album set of the Broadway production of "Beatlemania") and good (an album by the Rutles, a parallel universe Beatles created by Eric Idle and Neil Innes).

MAGICAL HISTORY TOUR

by Jerry Lazar

Let's confess right up front here that when it comes to the Beatles a bigger sucker than me will not be found. Friends will flip through my albums, come to Harrison's *Wonderwall* or Lennon's *Two Virgins* . . . and you should see the looks. At least, I rationalize, I own only three of the twenty-odd virtually identical *Let It Be* bootlegs, and I never got duped into buying albums of Beatles songs by rip-off groups like the Liverpools. OK. OK. So I did shell out good money for *Best of The Beatles*, having been conned by the pre-Ringo shot of the group on the cover and a list of song titles that nobody had ever heard of. Talk about your first-on-the-block! As you probably know, the drummer in those days was a gent name of Pete Best. And this is his solo album. Get it? *Best* of the Beatles? I've since seen him on *What's My Line?*, where I was pleased to discover that he's become a baker in Liverpool. Good for you, Petey! I've hung onto your album, though; quite a little collector's item, isn't it? That and *Wonderwall*.

By now, of course, I've figured out where to draw the line on these matters. A fan, yes; a fanatic, no. For instance, you won't find me plunking down $15 to see this Broadway play (!) *Beatlemania*, or any other artificial imitation Beatle-flavored product. Nonetheless, the show has found its market; it has just opened in Los Angeles and supposedly has plans to clone itself all over the place. Clive Davis' Arista Records has even brought out an $11.98 *Beatlemania* double album, which bears the warning: "An incredible simulation." (Look up the meaning of "incredible" when you get a chance.) I haven't heard the album, but I'll bet anything it sounds quite a bit like the Liverpools, as I remember them. They, too, made my teeth itch.

No need to despair, though, for there *are* a few new Beatle bargains to be had. One is the complete *A Hard Day's Night* screenplay, recently published by Penguin Books ($6.95). I was overjoyed to see it — not for its shot-by-shot stills, not for its lengthy interview with director Richard Lester, but for its page 62. There, as I had been trying to tell everyone for years, is the scene, right near the beginning, in which Lennon is *snorting a bottle of Coke*. In 1964! How hip! How cool! How ahead! I was ecstatic.

Even bigger treats are to be found in the genre of revisionism. When I came across the book *Paperback Writer* last spring, I didn't realize at first it was a novel, because it was subtitled *A New History Of The Beatles*. But the author's disclaimer was the tip-off: "Just because there'll never be another Beatles doesn't necessarily mean there can't be another Beatles' *story*." Early in the first chapter we read the part about a young plumber named Brian Epstein who is called in late one night to repair a clogged pipe in the ladies room at the Cavern. From there we get a fairly funny account of the four rockers as we *might have* known and loved them. The plane of reality is tilted at odd angles:

Dylan instructs a worshipful Lennon and a cynical McCartney in the art of writing lyrics: "Words and phrases . . . the first thing that comes to your mind . . . I don't even know what my songs mean." The result of the trio's collaboration is "Pneumonia Ceilings," typed on London Hilton stationery — except for the last line, which everyone is too stoned to remember.

Backstage at the Sullivan show, George tries out a new song for Del Shannon, who wasn't even aware that George wrote any: "Sounds to me like that song the Chiffons had out last year," comments Shannon. "Sounds just like it. Same changes."

Mark Shipper, the author, is a 28-year-old assistant publisher of a weekly trade paper, *Radio and Records*. He tapped out *Paperback Writer* in six weeks and, investing his own savings, printed 500 copies, which he tried to sell by mail order for $5.95 a pop. One copy came to the attention of Fred Jordan, who now has his own imprint at Grosset & Dunlap. Jordan plans to publish it as a large-format trade paperback in June. He's billing it as the first real rock novel ever written, but Shipper is more realistic. "It's just meant to be fun," he says.

Then we have the Rutles. You heard right: the Rutles. Ron Nasty, Dirk McQuickly, Stig O'Hara and Barry Wom — otherwise known as the Pre-fab Four. If you don't already know their tale — "the legend that will last a lunchtime" — then you can tune in on March 22 to NBC's documentary *All You Need Is Cash*, which was filmed last summer by Eric Idle and Gary Weis. *Saturday Night Live* and Monty Python meet the Beatles. Sort of.

Idle — who created, wrote and narrates the program — is Rutle bassist McQuickly. Neil Innes, of Bonzo Dog Band fame, wrote the lyrics and composed the Rutles tunes. (He's also Lennon sound-alike Ron Nasty.) Rikki Fataar, who once toured with the Beach Boys, is Stig. John Halsey, whom I never heard of before, is drummer Barry. A handful of the *Saturday Night* crew have cameo parts, and even

Mick Jagger and Paul Simon were persuaded to come on camera to describe what effect the Rutles had on *their* careers.

Mark Shipper and Eric Idle have separately and independently recreated the Beatles era using roughly the same idiom, if not the same medium. Shipper puts his Beatles through episodes that, had this been an even zanier world, *might* have happened. He rewrites Beatles lyrics and titles. Idle goes one step further: he changes *all* the names; and Innes rewrites the music as well. It doesn't sound like a particularly funny concept (or even an original one; remember AM deejays cracking themselves up by singing "I Wanna Hold My Nose"?), but it works. It works because of its underlying attitude: it's not analytical or imitative or grandiose. It's just meant to be fun.

I find myself telling skeptical friends to be sure to catch this special, and I try to give them an idea of what makes the Rutles so good by singing one of their songs, like "Get Up and Go" (the "Get Back" takeoff) or, better, "OUCH!" the title cut of their second movie. ("Ouch! Please don't hurt me. Ouch! Don't desert me. Ouch!") Neil Innes has managed to capture the Beatles' sound as convincingly as Todd Rundgren did on his *Faithful* album, and with more purpose. Enriching the spoof of the Beatles (and of our collective reaction to them) is a marvelous send-up of the entire genre of television documentaries: their cost, language and camera techniques.

Watching the Rutles, one is struck by the number of Beatle images that have permanently implanted themselves in our brainpans and by how accurately they are recreated here. Film editor Aviva Slesin, who put in three months of 14-hour days on this project, has done a masterful job of capturing the madness and bounciness of the original Richard Lester films; and the *Yellow Submarine* parody is indistinguishable from the real thing. Even the press conference sequences do justice to their prototypes. (Q: "Did you feel better after seeing the Queen?" A: "No. I feel better after seeing a doctor.")

Of course, it's tough to ridicule the inherently ridiculous. Sometimes real life can't be topped: Paul getting a hit single out of "Mary Had a Little Lamb" or George getting convicted of plagiarism. How do you beat that? When the Rutles try to go real life one better, it doesn't always work. I mean, why show John and Yoko holding forth for peace in a shower? Wasn't a bed absurd enough?

Meanwhile, George and Ringo are teaming up for a TV special which is being touted as (good Christ!) a musical version of *The Prince and the Pauper*. I can't figure which is worse, this or the idea of a 1978 Beatles album with tunes like "Disco Yoko," "Disco Love Songs," "My Sweet Disco" and Ringo's remake of "Disco

197

Duck." I'm so glad the band packed it in when it did.

Now I'm a newly converted sucker for the Rutles. Their first (and last) album has just been released, and it's the genuine item. Where have these guys been all these years?

Introduction to
PEOPLE AND THINGS
THAT WENT BEFORE

The three previous articles in this unit addressed fan conventions, bootleg recordings and memorabilia collecting, all staples of Beatlemania in the decade after the group's disbandment. A fourth, the long philosophical look back is tackled by Patrick Snyder in "People and Things That Went Before."

First published in the June 1973 issue of *Crawdaddy*, the essay assesses the impact of the Beatles through a historical retelling of their story.

PEOPLE AND THINGS
THAT WENT BEFORE

by Patrick Snyder

A kerosene-soaked and rag-wrapped wooden cross jutted out of the summer weeds and stood outlined against the curve of the dark South Carolina sky. In the harsh ground level glare of forty headlamps, white-hooded men in long ghostly cloaks formed a broad circle around their crude Christian icon. One man, dressed not in white but in gleaming lizard green that glimmered like molten emeralds when he moved, walked through the circle and up to the cross. He took a twelve-inch lp to which no one there had ever listened and fastened it securely to the crossbar where it intersected the six-foot upright. As the Grand Dragon tightened the wire around the record, kerosene squeezed from the rags and ran over his rough workingman's hands. Stopping first to wipe the oily fuel from his forty-year callouses, he took a torch, lit it with his Navy Zippo and touched it to the base of the cross.

The pale circle cheered as smokey orange flames leapt and curled under the now-sinking moon. At first, the record seemed unaffected by the hot halo of fire that surrounded it but then it buckled and began to melt, dripping globs of sooty plastic onto the red, cotton-sucked earth. The label on the crucified disc peeled and burned, and the words "The Beatles" crumbled into ashes and were carried away by the swift night wind.

The year was 1966 and John Lennon has said that his band was more popular than Jesus. He was right and this cracker *auto de fey* came much too late to turn the tide. These proud, parochial Southerners had lost their children's hearts to four creepy-haired *boys* from England and it had begun to hurt. In general, most of America smirked condescendingly at this fiery fundamentalist denunciation and the others like it that August, not realizing that these men with their molasses drawls and hip pocket hooch were *right*. The Beatles presented every bit the threat to the future America had designed for its children that the Klan said they did. But who then could have known that only a year later one of their records would convince a generation to smoke pot and try LSD? Why did it happen? How did The Beatles capture and hold the imagination of so many young people for so long that they became the relentless catalysts of a complex set of social changes that would rework the facade of the Western world?

the people in the cheap seats clap . . .

After World War II, nature repopulated the earth in a burst of fertility that was to provide The Beatles with their primary audience. In the United States, these young men and women, five to ten years younger than The Beatles themselves, began to experience the tenor of society around 1960. For the first time, a man who was not yet old was elected President and he made it respectable to be young. John Kennedy addressed his most idealistic pronouncements to the youth and, in contrast to the calcified mummy he succeeded, he symbolized an America reborn and promised an era of greatness and joy.

The Kennedy administration created for the youth, too immature to perceive political realities, a psychic environment that reverberated with all the great myths of American life. A new frontier was proclaimed and the young President/pioneer rode out into it with hydrogen six-guns to conduct Gunsmoke diplomacy that called upon the holy macho virtues of steely nerve and lightning reflexes. However, it was a game for the highest of stakes and everyone felt that too; the threat of nuclear holocaust permeated the atmosphere with gut-wrenching immediacy. The omnipresence of the possibility of complete annihilation created in the young an unfocused fatalism that was reflected in the tone of much of the music they bought and listened to. Song after song romantically recounted the story of young lovers separated by the fateful hand of untimely death.

Perhaps "The Last Kiss" was a harbinger of the perfect media smooch in Dallas? Kennedy's assassination shook the very foundations of the American reality the youth had so wholeheartedly embraced. It was a national trauma capped by three days of coast-to-coast televised mourning that punctured the American mythos and left many of the young disillusioned and lost.

The week before the assassination, *Time* ran a story on a bizarre phenomenon sweeping Great Britain called, of all things, The Beatles. A pop vocal group with gimmick hairstyles, they generated more excitement and hysteria than anyone had since Elvis. These four rather sallow workingclass kids from Liverpool with bad teeth were blessed with a cheeky wit and an infectious exuberance, but *Time* assured us the music they made was little more than noise. From wearing ridiculous collarless suits to putting on frenetic stage shows, they readily

202

admitted that they were only in it for the money. *Time* tsked and marched on.

However, the Luce-punning rag hadn't reckoned with Brian Epstein's promotional abilities, Ed Sullivan's showbusiness acumen or, most importantly, the amazing power of The Beatles' music. "I Want to Hold Your Hand" smashed into the pubescent underbelly of America a month and a half later with the impact of a fuel-injected linebacker on ups and poppers. With voices swimming gleefully on top of beat-heavy music, it sent electric chills scampering over every inch of Clearasiled female skin in the nation. And there were half a dozen more songs, each with the same power to totally absorb the adolescent consciousness into their positive romantic reality.

In the negative, disoriented reality of America in January, 1964, The Beatles became a safety valve for the release of trauma-wrought tensions. They replaced a ruptured American dream with a new dream that valued love, and holding hands, and dancing with you above all else. Peter, Paul and Mary, The Kingston Trio and the Brothers Four, with their songs of gentle protest and bittersweet romance, simply disappeared from the singles market; their lilting melodies and literary lyrics could simply not match the nimble energy of the Beatles.

By the time February rolled around, Beatlemania had seized the nation and 75% of its television sets tuned in to Ed Sullivan to get a glimpse of the four young men responsible for all this furor. Out they came, John ("Sorry girls, he's married"), Paul, George and Ringo, and unlike the previous decade's pop idols, they didn't seem the least bit dangerous or licentious. In fact, they were cute with their happy grins and spiffy suits that seemed a bit too small. Of course, their hair was totally outrageous and carefully lubricated pompadours all over America became fluffy bangs overnight.

For months afterward, The Beatles were responsible for centuries of after-school detention as they fueled endless panting discussions in studyhalls and classrooms all over America. The insides of locker doors were plastered with their pictures and radios and record players (what's a stereo?) blasted their music almost constantly. Amidst the Beatle hours, the Beatle days, and even the Beatle weeks (very difficult with less than two dozen songs), you would tune in each Friday to find out if your favorite was number one this time around. Singlehandedly, they accounted for 60% of the retail record sales in the top hundred, including positions one through five.

The Beatles crested a wave of pop trends in England that had been at work for half a decade or more. As the once globe-girdling British Empire began to dissolve and the United Kingdom became more and more dependent on the wealth and power of the United

States, the country's rigid class system began to crumble, allowing workingclass blood to flow into and revitalize the arts. In film, a whole movement emerged based on the techniques of the English documentary tradition and the aesthetics of the neo-realists. Directors like Lindsay Anderson, Jack Clayton and Tony Richardson made films about the workingclass and used its sons and daughters, like Albert Finney and Rita Tushington, to act in them. As part of the theatrical renaissance, satirical revues such as "Beyond the Fringe" gained great popularity and reflected the irreverent working-class attitudes that were to make The Beatles' quips to the press so eminently quotable.

Continually poking gentle fun at themselves and their success (John: "When I feel my head start to swell, I look at Ringo and know perfectly well we're not supermen"), The Beatles avoided the hypocritical posturing that was the norm for most previous pop-stars. They never issued saccharine homilies about brushing your teeth or being nice to Mum and Dad. They admitted they enjoyed making the money that was cascading into their coffers from all over the world, but refused to take themselves or the adulation of their fans seriously. And making money was the one thing we had all been taught to take seriously. In some ways, this could be taken as an extension of the early '60s Pop Art sensibility that had, by elevating the images of soup cans and coke bottles to the level of fine art seriousness, denied the seriousness of everything. The music the Beatles so prolifically created evolved from an amalgam of influences. The idea of a singing *and* playing group (virtually unique in an era when American performers were generally one or the other) had roots in their boyhood skiffle days. Weaned on rock and roll from the States, The Beatles reflected bits and pieces of all the genres that music had subdivided into, from The Everly Brothers to The Marvelettes with stops at Elvis, Little Richard and Buddy Holly. Holding the faceted mirror of their own creativity and cultural environment up to American rock, they broke it into its component parts and bounced back a music that was unlike any of it but similar to all of it.

Albert Grossman described The Beatles' primary accomplishment as making it "okay to be white." England had no indigenous black community and therefore no indigenous black music to be ripped off by whites searching for a visceral thrill. Rock and roll, to the English, came on as a gestalt of black music (blues and rhythm and blues), white music (folk and country) and all the various hybrids of the two. The Beatles brewed a mixture the Americans could never have concocted themselves because their inculcated prejudices, both in taste and in race, would not allow it. The Beatles openly expressed their admiration for "colored American groups" and opened their

204

Stateside audiences to a rich domestic tradition of music they probably would have permanently ignored.

In one swift year, The Beatles revitalized rock and gave it new standards and directions. First, they made excellent music, given the often primitive confines of rock in that era, writing much of it themselves and interpreting a wide range of other people's material. They performed this music with a raw energy they had perfected in Hamburg and an effervescent elan that flowed from their own fascinating personalities. Second, they spearheaded the "British Invasion" that in the next year introduced a whole galaxy of English artists reworking American forms, like The Animals who set more than a few folk purists back on their acoustic heels with their relentlessly powerful interpretation of the blues classic, "House of the Rising Sun." And third, they inspired, by example, a host of American imitators who would soon create great music of their own. The Beatles standardized the rock ensemble — two guitars, bass and drums — eschewing (for the time being) brass in general and the saxophone in particular, and relegating the piano and organ to subsidiary positions. Around this basic mix of instruments many fine American folk musicians, whom the Beatles had recently convinced of the amplifier's emotive power, organized their bands. The Byrds and The Mamas and Papas always owed the rock half of their folk/rock form directly to the Beatles, and in 1965, even Dylan went electric.

Throughout The Beatles' careers, their output was surrounded by expanding rings of influence on the artists working around them, but their paramount accomplishment will always be the music they made themselves. From the very beginning until almost the end of their existence as a group, they continually managed to improve on their previous efforts, becoming more and more innovative and original each step of the way. They even made considerable progress between their first album (The Veejay material in the U.S.) and their second, *Meet the Beatles*. The first time out their results were rather childish and subdued, but by the second round in the studio George Martin had learned how to capture the rocking excitement of their live act on record. It's the difference between the sing-song preciousness of "Do You Want To Know A Secret" and the sustained energy of "All My Loving."

For the first two years, until *Help!*, The Beatles wrote essentially the same kind of songs, although they included many diverse types: up-tempo ravers like "Can't Buy Me Love," exercises in r&b funk like "You Can't Do That," and gentle lovely ballads like "And I Love Her." All of them fell into categories that existed before and were performed with only elaborations on established rock techniques. Minor innovations like the feedback intro to "I Feel Fine" crept in, but on *Help!* they began a series of successful explorations that

205

would ascend with ever-growing brilliance to their masterpiece two years later, *Sgt. Pepper's Lonely Hearts Club Band.*

By the time of *Help!* (1965),* The Beatles had perfected their pop rock form, turning out blissfully superb numbers like "You're Gonna Lose That Girl" at will. However, on other songs, they displayed an increasing sophistication of lyrical content and musical fluency. Lennon's "You've Got to Hide Your Love Away" examined for the first time the aching loneliness and alienation that would dominate so much of this later work, and for the first time introduced the verbal imagery of his two books into song. There John stood, head in hand, his face turned to the wall, as Paul sang his hauntingly beautiful "Yesterday" accompanied by that hallmark, until then, of Tin Pan Alley kitsch, strings. George introduced a little electronic gimmickry for the first time in "I Need You" when he distorted his chords with a simple volume peddle. Perhaps the most seminal cut on the album, "Ticket to Ride" pounded out with an electronic heaviness and ear-searing presence that convinced the whole of rock that the keynote of the future would be, very simply, get LOUDER.

Marijuana became a regular part of The Beatles' lives during the making of their second film, *Help!* (Also during the shooting of that film, George, bored between takes, picked up one of the props to amuse himself. It was a sitar.) Their next album, *Rubber Soul*, reflected both these new interests and, from the dark-toned, obliquely angled cover photo to the music inside, presented us with a subtly different Beatles. George's new-found sitar debuted on Lennon's poignantly understated "Norwegian Wood" in a perfect example of the creative crossfertilization that made the wide range of their advances possible. A number of attitudes surfaced for the first time that would play increasingly important roles in the years to come. "Nowhere Man," a rather bland song spiced with a glistening harmonic, was their first step toward obvious social commentary but with the incisive twist, "Isn't he a bit like you and me." However, "The Word" showed no sign of self-doubt. On the contrary, it

----

The albums referred to in this piece are the British versions which have 7 cuts per side. Capitol (with the U.S. standard of 6 cuts per side) used to save, until Sgt. Pepper, 2 cuts per album and, with the inclusion of singles which the Beatles rarely included on albums in England, create whole extra albums. Help! was a bonanza for Capitol, because in England the songs from the film filled one side while the other side was 7 new songs that eventually turned up in the U.S. on Beatles 6, Rubber Soul and the completely synthetic Yesterday & Today which also includes tracks from the original Rubber Soul and Revolver. Other than sheer pedantry, the reason I have based this piece on the original albums is that the Beatles' stylistic evolution is much more apparent through them. — P.S.

proclaimed the way to spiritual salvation, and then, in a crucial couplet, The Beatles appointed themselves its prophets.

Now that I know that view must be right
I'm here to show everybody the light.

It was so fine, sunshine: How could they resist informing the world? And The Beatles were in the unique position to do just that. They had rocketed to a pinnacle of success and popularity from which they had immediate access to the minds of a whole generation.

Both "Paperback Writer" and "Rain," their next single, continued the maturity *Rubber Soul* had revealed. "Paperback" wittily attacked artless hacks (newspaper taxis?) and subtly suggested it was themselves they were talking about when it borrowed "Frere Jacques" for the background vocal. "Rain" pointed toward the dense, electronic sound they would strive for in the future as it alternately glided over and pummeled the listener with waves of churning sound that glinted with Harrison's whining Indian-influenced lead. It faded out and then returned backwards to presage the tape loop collages to come.

Simultaneously with the release of two songs that could not be reproduced in concert, "Eleanor Rigby" and "Yellow Submarine," The Beatles permanently abandoned the grind of touring and the hysteria of their live performances. Appropriately, their last appearance was in San Francisco, August, 1966, the city that had become the focal point of a furious new bubbling in the underground. Kesey's maniac trips festivals had announced a new, freeflowing mass encounter, media-scorched psychedelic experience that differed radically from the solemn spirituality of Leary's east coast explorations. San Francisco had donned a day-glo striped and strobe-studded cloak and The Beatles followed suit as they prepared to move from the smokey seductiveness of *Revolver* to the piebald pirouetting wonder of *Sgt. Pepper*.

However, a long gestation period was required and for a while The Beatles either dropped out of sight or went their separate ways. In the United States, where Capitol had released fifteen singles in two years, (as opposed to the nine they had released in England during the same period), rumors flew that they were breaking up. Paul wrote the music for *A Family Way*, George journeyed to India with his wife, and John played a supporting role in Lester's *How I Won the War*. The musical seeds The Beatles had sown had begun to grow and flower, and it seemed that their years of absolute dominance were over. From back home in England, The Rolling Stones had staked out an area of hard-edged raunch and made it their own. Dylan had released his monumental *Blonde on Blonde* while Brian

Wilson demonstrated his melodic mastery of the recording studio with *Pet Sounds*. And in San Francisco a whole new generation of bands was crawling out of a hilly womb with music by and for the graduates of the acid test.

The audience had changed too, growing toward a maturity unlike any other the world had seen. Their nervous systems had been linked since childhood to a system of communications that made events on the other side of the globe palpably real and immediate. Educated in a system that encourages self-inquiry, their minds searched for new meanings and justifications. They were still young, and soft, and malleable but the bud contained a new flower that would blossom soon.

Then the absent Beatles sent a cryptic message, an invitation to a place called Strawberry Fields where nothing was real and there was nothing to get hung about. On the other side, they celebrated the simple joys of life on Penny Lane. These glowing aural arrows pointed to a place across an horizon we had only barely sensed, but these were the same voices that had accompanied our adolescence with their energy and life. Why should we begin to doubt them now?

After more months of quiet, at the beginning of the Summer *Newsweek* called Love, it came and everyone followed. With eight Beatles on the cover, *Sgt. Pepper* swept into our lives like a cyclone. The album compelled you to listen in a whole new way because it was a coherent cycle of songs that illuminated a series of interrelated but individually stunning vignettes. It took all of the impulses and emotions that had been stirring in the garrets of New York and the parks of San Francisco and pumped them out into the world. On an implicit level to which the young people intuitively connected, it offered an alternative set of values based on generational ethnocentrism and the fellowship of the psychedelic sacrament. But explicitly, it was simply a splendid time guaranteed for all.

Without doubt, *Sgt. Pepper* was the most influential record album ever released. In three months, it sold two and a half million copies, permanently changing rock's emphasis from the single to the album, as it cracked open the doors of perception for all those who sat blissfully enthralled in its intricate tapestry of images and sounds. In December of 1967, 60% of American college students identified this album and/or John Lennon as the single most important influence of their lives. From a pop podium of unequaled prominence, The Beatles promulgated a subversive vision to a ready-made audience of millions of fertile young minds. The result was metaphysical Beatlemania, the same sort of frenzied devotion that had occurred in '64, on a much more sophisticated level.

The new role The Beatles assumed on *Sgt. Pepper*, as artist/messiahs chronicling their age, was transferred, for better and worse, to the music in general. In an environment shot through with the first rushes of acid optimism, we turned to our electric troubadors for answers to the most profound of questions, and our budding minds burst forth into flowers that grew so incredibly high.

. . . the rest of you can rattle your jewelry

In early 1964, Brian Epstein was offered over $300,000 for the agency rights to The Beatles. He would have maintained personal management but with ultimate control over only their personal activities. Already feeling the strain of day to day business dealings, he presented the idea to the boys. John replied, "Get stuffed!" and they threatened to break up if he sold them. Epstein's role in their career was much more than that of a business major domo; he was a friend, entranced by their charismatic genius, who provided the best possible atmosphere for the fulfillment of their creativity. When he died in 1967, that group creativity began to falter and the fissures that would eventually divide them began to appear.

From this point on they would be plagued by the problems of organizing the vast business empire their success had created. As John drifted into himself to battle the devils that were the price of his genius, Paul, always the most conservative in lifestyle, filled the vacuum in leadership and direction left by Brian's death with his energy and ideas. The others, although unwilling or unable to balance his energy with their own, chafed under Paul's direction.

Intoxicated with their success in the recording studio, The Beatles tried to similarly conquer the twentieth century's other great technological art form, film, and it lead to their first real failure. Following the Merry Pranksters' example, they set out in a gaily-painted bus to create a television film as they meandered through the English countryside. When it was finished and dubbed *Magical Mystery Tour*, it received universally negative reviews. However, the music they created for it and as singles to follow *Sgt. Pepper*, continued their streak of brilliant recordings. "I Am the Walrus," beating with its siren rhythm, filled the air with a turgid wail that was the obverse of the rainbow vision they had so recently depicted.

After Sexy Sadie (the Maharishi) had made a bit of a fool of everyone, The Beatles announced the formation of their ridiculously utopian corporate umbrella, Apple, and staffed it with friends less capable and less genuine than Brian.

Unfortunately, *Sgt. Pepper* proved to be a peak rather than the beginning of a long plateau of greatness. All of the most aesthetically profound directions it had hinted at were never again explored. The transformation of the album, as a form, from a collection to a cycle of songs was pursued only once more and then only as a medley for part of one side. When George realized he could never become even a mediocre sitarist by *Indian* standards, the strong Eastern influence in his music evaporated forever. And most importantly, the fusion of rock and contemporary classical music (as exemplified by Cage and Stockhausen) that *Pepper* and "Walrus" alluded to was also abandoned. With the absolute technical expertise, both in recording and composing, they had garnered over the years, The Beatles produced the disquieting white album. Without doubt it had its moments — "Blackbird," "While My Guitar Gently Weeps" and "Dear Prudence" with its summerbreeze voices and chiming guitars — but it indicated a lack of internal discipline and an unwillingness to create communally. No longer were the burrs and slivers of their individual visions honed by a group consciousness to form a coherent and complementary mosaic. Instead, we were served Paul with The Beatles, John with The Beatles, and George with The Beatles in an overgrown, unfocused mass.

Their fifteen-year-old union of boys was not surviving the transition to manhood: their tastes, especially John's and Paul's, and their interests began to diverge more and more. With the constant hassles of business besieging their creative lives, The Beatles, as a group of communal artists, could not evolve naturally out of its established forms and concepts of itself. With *Sgt. Pepper*, they announced they had moved beyond being everybody's faverave pop group but now they could find no way of being anything other than their own faverave pop group. George discovered that there was simply no room in The Beatles for his now prolific outpouring of material, and John found the others resenting Yoko and his enrapturement with her grapefruit ice cream koans.

Throughout the late '60s, Beatle singles continued to burst over the music business like flares. "Hey Jude," "Lady Madonna," "Get Back," "Don't Let Me Down" and "Let It Be" all had their moment of excellence and months of influence but the essential, intangible chemistry necessary for the successful completion of a major project had disappeared. The brilliant crystal that had gathered the scattered light of its times and refracted it into a single shining beam had broken down into its component atoms and the energy needed to refuse it was simply no longer available.

At Paul's urging, and hoping for past lightning to strike again, they embarked on the ambitious and abortive *Let It Be* movie/album. Supposedly they were going to become The Beatles again in the process and go out on tour, fulfilling the mythic legacy that bound them together as a single being in four parts. But the myth had become a prison and its chains were leaving deep welts in their flesh. The film emerged finally as a grainy testament to their dissolution; the album, salvaged or butchered by Phil Spector depending on your

210

point of view, finally proved they were human; and the tour ended up as 45 minutes on a London rooftop.

With *Let It Be* still a mass of half-hearted tapes, The Beatles went into the studio and quickly recorded their largest-selling album, *Abbey Road*. It includes some of Lennon and Harrison's strongest individual material, "Something" and "Come Together," but *Abbey Road*, like the white album, overwhelms the listener more with its technical magnificence than with the depth of its feeling. The second side's terribly impressive but ultimately fraudulent medley is little more than a series of interesting but unrealized song fragments artificially impregnated with one another. You can sit in this armchair and feel their disease.

Extravagant mismanagement had finally upset the Apple cartel sometime before *Abbey Road* and an outsider became necessary to save it. The conclusive rupture came over whether that outsider would be Paul's candidate or John's, and the end, with its boiling invective, and frigid lawsuits, was ugly. On their own, they have produced predictably: Ringo made one album of "What Goes On" and another of "Goodnight"; George became a superstar sideman, recorded an album touched with brilliance and plagued by self-consciousness, and then organized the holiest event in the history of rock and roll; Paul became a self-satisfied and probably quite happy (ham)burgher as his music degenerated into frivolous trivialities; and John created one pain-gnawed and totally idiosyncratic masterpiece and two albums whose flashes of poetry make their polemics that much more distasteful.

Of late, rumors of a resurrection have echoed through the land, especially since the news of Allen Klein's curt dismissal. For the time being, immigration problems (they won't let McCartney in and they want Lennon out) seem to have intervened, but even a physical reunion under the best of conditions will have great difficulty in summoning the transcendent magic that made them so special. They were lightning rods grounding the energy of their times. Whatever their future(s) might be and however sour the last taste was, it can never tarnish the treasury of music The Beatles created along the way. A finely woven garment whose seams are more visible now that we've seen its tailor work alone, the music can still enfold you in its beauty, wit, and insight. The Beatles were a moving window that allowed us to glimpse dreams and realities that without their lens might have remained forever obscured.

[Editor's note: Realizing that his 1973 proclamations about the Beatles' significant and enduring place in world history might have been a bit too bold and unrealistic, Patrick Snyder here offers a 1983 postscript to his personal memoir:

"A footnote to history they are, but to myself and my peers they will remain much more. As evidence of this, I found my throat tightening and my jaw clenching each of the two times John Lennon was shown in clips on the most recent Grammy Awards show. Lennon, now sacrificed and martyred, holds a very special place. His death is very difficult for me to reconcile and most of my friends of my age agree with me. I recently asked a 26 year old if he felt anything particularly strong when Lennon died. He said, 'No, not really, no more than others.' For me, the answer is the opposite: 'Yes, really, more than others. Much more.' I am puzzled by the depth of the emotion and the sharpness of the sense of loss I still experience. I had counted on growing old with old John around. So, for me, The Beatles are still fascinating and problematic. They gave shape and excitement to my adolescence; sent me off searching out things that I might never have looked into . . . and, most important, they challenged me and made me think. I feel lucky to have had them."]

FURTHER READING
PART V

Were the Beatles really as great as all their fans want everyone to think they were? Nine music critics square off on that question in "Nine Ways of Looking at the Beatles, 1963–1973" (by Eric Salzman, Joel Vance, Noel Coppage, Lester Bangs, Richard Goldstein, John Mendelsohn, Nat Hentoff, Patrick Carr and Lillian Roxon, *Stereo Review*, February 1973, pages 57–63). The results are predictable: five yea and four nay, but the article is worth hunting down. Lillian Roxon, the late author of the *Rock Encyclopedia*, concludes the discussion with a look at young fans too young to remember the early Beatles. She suggests, among other things, that press agent Derek Taylor should write a book, Cynthia Lennon could start a lecture tour of high schools and someone should open a Beatles museum in Times Square. Derek Taylor did write his book (see "Further Reading, Part I"). Cynthia Lennon Twist, although not yet on the high school circuit, wrote her autobiography, *A Twist of Lennon* (Avon Books, 1978) and appeared at the New York City "Beatlefest" in September, 1981. No Beatles museum has been established in Times Square, but across the ocean is the Cavern Mecca at 18 Mathew Street, Liverpool, near the former location of the famous Cavern Club, where the Beatles performed in their youth.

Planning a trip to Liverpool . . . to London? *The Beatles' England* (910 Press, 1982), by David Bacon and Norman Maslov, should be a handy reference for anyone wishing to visit the locations made famous by Beatles lore.

Closely related to the subject of bootleg recordings, the article "Resurrecting the Beatles: Star-Club to Stereo," by Charles Repka, *High Fidelity Magazine* (August 1977, pages 101–103), recounts the work of producer Larry Grossberg to reproduce an amateur recording of an early Beatles performance for the stereo LP **The Beatles Live! at the Star-Club in Hamburg, Germany: 1962**.

Two long-awaited guides to collecting Beatles memorabilia appeared in 1982. *The Beatles: A Collection* (Robcin Associates, 1982), by Robert and Cindy DelBuono, is a photographic catalog and pricing guide. And *Collecting the Beatles* (Pierian Press, 1982), by Barbara Fenick, includes tips on buying and collecting along with photos and going rates.

In *The Beatles on Record* (Charles Scribner's Sons, 1982), J.P. Russell gives an in-depth, track-by-track analysis of each Beatles LP, including names of session men, pertinent historical information and data on songs recorded but never released. He even details odd parts of songs not credited on album covers and utterances and other non-musical sounds between songs.

Russell's work is joined by a book of the same title, *The Beatles on Record* (Fireside, 1982), by Mark Wallgren. Wallgren features photos of each Beatles single and LP released in the United States, including solo efforts and reissues. A short chart history accompanies each disk, and even singles released in plain sleeves are pictured with much of the label copy very legible.

Body Count (by Francie Schwartz, a former live-in girlfriend of Paul McCartney, Straight Arrow Books, 1972) told a little. *Lennon Remembers* (John's 1970 interview with *Rolling Stone* editor Jann Wenner, Fawcett Popular Library, 1972) told a lot. But apparently they did not tell enough. In *The Love You Make* (McGraw-Hill, 1983), former Beatles assistant Peter Brown (with Steven Gaines) reveals some very shocking insider insights of the Beatles' private lives. More to come?

This editor has received some pre-publication criticism for not including an essay on John Lennon in *The Beatles Reader*. John Lennon's story is deserving of its own anthology, and that work has been produced by the editors of *Rolling Stone*. *The Ballad of John and Yoko* (Rolling Stone/Doubleday/Dolphin, 1982) combines over thirty essays, interviews and personal recollections in this marvelous collection edited by Jonathan Cott and Christine Doudna.